200 PRAYERS OF STRENGTH FOR MEN

COURAGE FOR TROUBLED TIMES

BARBOUR
PUBLISHING

© 2024 by Barbour Publishing, Inc.

Editorial assistance by Elijah Adkins

ISBN 978-1-63609-751-0

Scripture quotations are taken from the Barbour Simplified KJV, copyright © 2022 by Barbour Publishing, Inc., Uhrichsville, Ohio 44683. All rights reserved.

Cover Design: Greg Jackson, Thinkpen Design

Published by Barbour Publishing, Inc., 1810 Barbour Drive, Uhrichsville, Ohio 44683, www.barbourbooks.com

Our mission is to inspire the world with the life-changing message of the Bible.

Member of the
Evangelical Christian
Publishers Association

Printed in China.

200 PRAYERS OF STRENGTH FOR MEN:

COURAGE FOR TROUBLED TIMES

These inspiring prayers and scripture selections will turn your eyes from the troubles of this world to the far greater power and glory of your great God.

Based on passages from scripture—in the fresh yet familiar Barbour Simplified King James Version—these prayers offer a powerful jolt of spiritual truth for your daily challenges. There's even a topical index to direct you right to the prayers you need most!

With *200 Prayers of Strength for Men*, you'll be on your way to more meaningful, purposeful, honest conversation with your mighty Creator—who hears your every prayer.

THE BLESSED LIFE

Blessed is the man who does not walk in the counsel of the ungodly or stand in the way of sinners or sit in the seat of the scornful. But his delight is in the law of the LORD, and on His law he meditates day and night.

PSALM 1:1–2

Father of all blessings, every day I encounter ideas and philosophies that try to compete with You and Your written Word for my attention. At best, these things are worldly distractions; at worst, they directly contradict Your teachings. Please help me to stay focused on the blessed promises, commandments, and encouragements in the Bible. Lord, make me hungrier every day for Your Word. Help me to make Bible reading and meditation as much a part of my day as eating, drinking, and breathing.

LIGHT MAKES A DIFFERENCE

For you were sometimes darkness, but now you are light in the Lord. Walk as children of light (for the fruit of the Spirit is in all goodness and righteousness and truth), proving what is acceptable to the Lord.
EPHESIANS 5:8–10

Lord, this world feels very dark sometimes, and I wonder if I'm making any difference at all. I want to shine brightly for You, but there are days, I confess, when I feel surrounded by murky shadows intent on bringing me down. That's why I'm so grateful for this reminder in Your Word that I belong to You—that it's really *Your* light I'm shining. As I step out into this big world, give me creative ideas so that I can shine in a way that draws others to You. I praise You for the joy of making a change, Lord.

A PERSONAL PRAYER

"And this is life eternal, that they might know You, the only true God, and Jesus Christ whom You have sent."
JOHN 17:3

In this prayer, heavenly Father, I want to speak to You about myself. I pray that it isn't a selfish prayer, for my ultimate goal is to be right with You. Please steer me away from sin and help me to accept Your forgiveness when I do sin. I long to be right with You. Direct my steps to always be in the path of righteousness.

Father, help me recognize the work You've given me and assist me as I try to glorify You. Stamp Your name on my heart so that I may live eternally in Your presence.

SATURATED

I will praise You, O Lord, with my whole heart; I will show forth all Your marvelous works. I will be glad and rejoice in You. I will sing praise to Your name, O You Most High.
PSALM 9:1–2

Almighty Father, when I stop and consider all the awesome things You've done for me, I'm overwhelmed with Your goodness. Sometimes, I get distracted by negative events and start forgetting how amazing You are and how much You love me. But all it takes is a moment of focusing on Your blessings, and I realize how You've saturated my life with good things. When people ask how I'm doing, give me courage to tell them how great You are. I'll keep a smile on my face and praise You today, Lord, for Your marvelous, mind-blowing love.

ALL-KNOWING

O the depth of the riches both of the wisdom and knowledge of God! How unsearchable are His judgments and His ways past finding out! "For who has known the mind of the Lord? Or who has been His counselor?"
Romans 11:33–34

You know, Lord! Even when I don't, You know all things about my journey—the road I should take, the decisions I should make, the plans You've established for me. You also know how to speak directly to my heart, guiding me every step of the way. You, my all-knowing Father, are the only one who truly has my best interest at heart. Today, I settle the issue once and for all: I trust *You* to lead me according to Your sovereign will.

DIVINE FORGETFULNESS

"And no longer shall every man teach his neighbor and every man his brother, saying, 'Know the LORD,' for they shall all know Me, from the least of them to the greatest of them," says the LORD. "For I will forgive their iniquity, and I will remember their sin no more."
JEREMIAH 31:34

God of forgiveness, it's so hard to imagine You being forgetful. Yet You've promised in this verse that once I've confessed my sins and received Your forgiveness, You wipe my past from Your mind, never to be remembered again. Lord, help me forget my mistakes and put my past behind me. I know You have. And who am I to hang on to things You've already chosen to forget?

PAYING IT FORWARD

*And God saw the light, that it was good, and
God divided the light from the darkness.*

GENESIS 1:4

One of the things I love most about You,
Lord, is that You always pay it forward. You
bless me abundantly and, in doing so, teach
me how I can bless others. Then, when I step
out and bless others, I know they will pass on
blessings in turn. What a powerful cycle—a
gift that keeps on giving. Show me how to pay
it forward in my everyday life—in both little
ways and big. I want to live adventurously,
always searching for new opportunities to
share Your light. Lord, it's so exciting to be
a blessing! I'm grateful to be used by You.

SETTING A COURSE

What man is he who fears the Lord? He shall instruct him in the way that he chooses.
PSALM 25:12

Lord, when the rain hits my windshield, I often see two raindrops fall only inches apart: one flows to the right, the other flows to the left.

Unlike the raindrops, I have the liberty to choose which direction my life flows. So heavenly Father, keep me from making careless judgments that can snowball into frightful consequences. Guide me away from the darkness of sin and into the light of righteousness. Give me Your wisdom for every choice I make. May my decisions always be based on the values I learn while studying Your Word.

SURPRISING LOVE

*Do not remember the sins of my youth
or my transgressions. According to Your
mercy remember me for Your goodness'
sake, O LORD. Good and upright is the LORD.
Therefore He will teach sinners in the way.*
PSALM 25:7–8

Dear Father, when I think of Your love for me, it blows my mind. I'm undeserving. I've made many mistakes, and I've broken many of Your laws. But Your love—it catches me by surprise, and I almost lose my breath. When You look at me, You don't see my past mistakes and failures. You see only Your cherished child. Thank You for viewing me through the lens of Your love. I want my entire life to be a continuous act of gratitude. But I can't do that without Your guidance and instruction. Today, Father, I'm giving You control. Show me how to be good like You.

YOU KNOW THE HEART

"Forgive, and act, and give to every man according to his ways, whose heart You know (for You, even You alone, know the hearts of all the children of men), that they may fear You all the days that they live in the land that You gave to our fathers."

1 KINGS 8:39–40

Lord, I question people all the time—wondering where their hearts are, why they do what they do, why they choose to hurt others, why they don't follow through on their promises. But such questions are pointless: only You know the motivations of others, and only You can speak to the deepest places in their hearts. I can trust You to know what's going on deep inside each of us. I praise You for that!

FINDING STRENGTH IN. . .WEAKNESS?

And He said to me, "My grace is sufficient for you, for My strength is made perfect in weakness." Therefore, I will boast most gladly even more in my weaknesses, that the power of Christ may rest on me.

2 CORINTHIANS 12:9

Mighty God, You know how we men think. You know we highly esteem physical and mental strength, and You know that weakness—in any form—is the last thing we want to admit. But Your Word tells me that whenever I acknowledge my weaknesses, I'm right where I belong. You want to empower me to do great things for You, but You also want me to acknowledge that I'm powerless without Your strength. So Lord, I embrace the fact that without You, I can't do anything.

COURAGEOUS FAITH

*Walk in wisdom toward those who
are without, redeeming the time.*
COLOSSIANS 4:5

Sometimes, when I wonder how I can make a difference in the world, Lord, You remind me that a key way to share the gospel is to stand up for what I believe. I'm surrounded by people and ideas that contradict my faith. It's overwhelming at times because these voices are so loud. They shout their beliefs in my ears and insist on being heard. Occasionally, I just want to cower and keep my mouth shut. But You're always opening doors for conversations, Lord. So with the courage of my convictions, help me step through these doors and speak truth in love, even when it's hard.

Can two walk together unless
they are agreed?
AMOS 3:3

Dear Lord, I'm disheartened by the many disagreements among Your children: fractured denominations, split congregations, and individuals who no longer speak to one another. Unfortunately, I confess that because of my own obstinacy, I've contributed to this lack of harmony.

Lord, I want to be more agreeable, not arrogant or unreasonable. Guide me to choose the right words that will lead to a better walk with You and with my brothers and sisters in Christ. Remind me that even if I'm right, I can still be wrong if my comments are not wrapped in love.

FAITH BUILDING

So then faith comes by hearing,
and hearing by the word of God.
ROMANS 10:17

Dear Father, I want to be a man of great faith. Rationally, I know Your promises. I know of Your power and love and greatness. I know nothing is impossible with You. But acting out that faith is a little harder. When giants loom, it's easy for me to surrender to fear— to forget all about Your power and focus on the size of the problem. But the answer to this lack of faith is to burrow deep in Your Word. As I fill my mind with Your wisdom, it becomes part of me. It shows up during the storm and pulls my attention back to You. Help me make Your Word a part of my daily routine as I work to build my faith.

FULL TO THE BRIM

For the earth shall be full of the knowledge of the Lord, as the waters cover the sea.
Isaiah 11:9

Father, what a grand picture You've painted with this verse. Your knowledge is so lofty that it's impossible for me to attain it. It's like an endless sea of mighty rushing waters, covering vast swaths of the entire planet. My thoughts are but a drop in comparison. But You invite me to share glimpses—to see that Your higher ways are better for me than my own. How could I ever doubt a God who sees all and knows all? I trust You, Lord.

FREE TO SERVE

For, brothers, you have been called to liberty; only do not use liberty for an occasion to the flesh, but by love serve one another. For all the law is fulfilled in one word, even in this: "You shall love your neighbor as yourself."

GALATIANS 5:13–14

Thank You, Jesus, for coming to earth to live and die and rise from the dead so that I could be freed from sin's terrible prison. Keep me from returning to that kind of bondage. I want to use my freedom to serve You and other people—not out of some need to atone for my wrongs but out of pure, humble, godly love. I'm free, so now I can move my focus away from myself and onto loving You and others. Thank You for freeing me.

TO THE WHOLE CREATION

And He said to them, "Go into all the world and preach the gospel to every creature."
MARK 16:15

Lord, I don't mind admitting that this verse is a little intimidating. It's hard enough to cross the street and talk to my neighbor about my faith—let alone to travel across the globe. But I know that You can and will use me in any situation, so I ask You today to do just that. You can create opportunities that are so natural that I don't even have to worry about what I'll say. You open doors of conversation with ease, Lord, and bid me to walk through them. May I never forget that every person I meet is someone for whom You died. Remembering that makes talking about You so much easier.

ENTER WITH THANKSGIVING

And God said to Moses, "I AM THAT I AM." And He said, "You shall say this to the children of Israel, 'I AM has sent me to you.' "
EXODUS 3:14

Father, I pray that I'll always enter Your presence in the proper way—in humble recognition that You are the Creator who called everything into existence. I bow in awe of You as I realize You are the I AM, the eternal presence that has spanned the ages. I cry to You as my provider and deliverer, and I gratefully acknowledge Your mercy, patience, and mindfulness toward me. I praise You for the blessings that flow from You.

HUMBLE AND STRONG

We, then, who are strong ought to bear the weaknesses of the weak, and not to please ourselves. Let every one of us please his neighbor for his good, for edification. For even Christ did not please Himself, but as it is written: "The reproaches of those who reproached You fell on Me."

ROMANS 15:1–3

Good Father, this scripture directly contradicts the world's selfish viewpoint. Human nature says we should please ourselves, but You tell us to put others first. The world sees humility as a weakness—like we're doormats—but You see it as a strength. Indeed, it takes character to set aside my own desires in favor of someone else's. Putting myself first only indicates that I'm weak and immature. Make me humble and strong, like You.

YET TO BE REVEALED

Beloved, now we are the sons of God, and it does not yet appear what we shall be, but we know that when He appears, we shall be like Him, for we shall see Him as He is.
1 JOHN 3:2

My vision is so cloudy, Lord, that I can't see what's coming around the next bend, let alone Your plans for the coming season of my life. Trusting You in such times is a bit like walking on water. When my own eyes feel unreliable and I feel like I'm going under, I know I can trust You, Father. You haven't let me drown yet. I'll keep my eyes on You.

PROPERLY MOTIVATED

"Be careful that you do not do your deeds of charity before men, to be seen by them. Otherwise you have no reward from your Father who is in heaven. Therefore when you do your deeds of charity, do not sound a trumpet before you, as the hypocrites do. . . . Truly I say to you, they have their reward."

MATTHEW 6:1–2

Lord Jesus, I know it's possible for me to do the right things for the wrong reasons. During Your earthly ministry, You taught Your followers to make certain that they never performed their good deeds or acts of charity in a way that brought attention to themselves. Remind me often to check my own heart to make sure that when I do good for others, my thoughts are on pleasing You first.

AN AUTHENTIC REFLECTION

*Only let your conduct be as is proper
for the gospel of Christ, that whether
I come and see you or else be absent,
I may hear of your affairs, that you stand
fast in one spirit, with one mind striving
together for the faith of the gospel.*

PHILIPPIANS 1:27

Lord, I want to be authentic. When people spend time with me in private, I want them to see the same person they see in public. No phony business. I never want my faith to be a turnoff to those who are watching. Instead, I want to bring honor to Your name, no matter the setting. I want them to be drawn to the Christ they see in me. Help me live this way, Lord. May I be a true reflection of You, attracting others toward Your kingdom.

THE IMPOSSIBLE

And He said, "The things that are impossible
with men are possible with God."
Luke 18:27

Father, some goals do appear unattainable to me. Yet I see that what was impossible even a hundred years ago has become possible today: space rockets, laptops, smartphones, and the internet were all once considered fanciful, wildly impractical, or impossible.

If these things can be done with the natural abilities You've given us, how much more is possible when You equip us to act in spiritual matters! Father, may the apparent unlikelihood of success never stop me from beginning a good work. Remind me that I am not acting alone—You are at my side. May my faith in You grow stronger each day.

BY FAITH

For I am not ashamed of the gospel of Christ, for it is the power of God for salvation to everyone who believes, to the Jew first and also to the Greek. For in it the righteousness of God is revealed from faith to faith, as it is written, "The just shall live by faith."

ROMANS 1:16–17

Holy God, Your gospel is what allows each of us to have a relationship with You. Because of the good news of salvation through Your Son, Jesus Christ, I can be righteous, or in right standing with You. The last part of this passage says, "The just shall live by faith." Do I live by faith? Or do my actions prove otherwise? Do I really believe all the things I say I believe? I want to. Teach me to let my actions match my words. Help me live by faith.

HOLY FEAR

Serve the LORD with fear and
rejoice with trembling.
PSALM 2:11

Holy God, this culture seems to respect You less and less each year. Even the church is filled with those who seemingly ignore and disregard Your Word, foolishly believing that You don't really care about the way we live. But Lord, I want to be different. I want my attitude toward You to be one of holy fear and reverence, not apathy or frustration. Teach me how to give You the respect that You deserve, almighty God. Show me how to obey Your rules and to love You with my soul, heart, and mind.

BEING A PRAYER WARRIOR

Epaphras, who is one of you, a servant of Christ, greets you, always laboring fervently for you in prayers, that you may stand perfect and complete in all the will of God.

COLOSSIANS 4:12

Father, Epaphras isn't one of the better-known men in the Bible. But how well he's known is far less important than what he's known for. Epaphras was a prayer warrior—a man willing to spend time before You on behalf of others—and Your Word honors him for that. Lord, I want to be that kind of man. I want to be someone who says, "I'll pray for you," and then follows through. More than that, though, I want You to see me as a man committed to coming to You every day in prayer for whatever You lay on my heart.

LOVE GIVES

"For God so loved the world that He gave His only begotten Son, that whoever believes in Him should not perish but have everlasting life."

JOHN 3:16

I'll never understand how You did it, Father—how You sent Your only Son to the earth to die for mankind. What an amazing, selfless sacrifice He made, offering His life in exchange for sinners across the globe. I've learned so much from Your example. More than anything, I've discovered that love gives and gives. . .and then gives some more. This sacrificial attitude flies in the face of our modern lifestyle. So many of us are in receiving mode, wanting our needs and wishes met right away. But You've shown me that in order to change the world, I need to be a giver. Search my heart, Lord. Make me more like You.

WALKING WITH YOU

Noah was a just man and perfect in his generations, and Noah walked with God.
GENESIS 6:9

Lord, I am defined by the heroes and role models I choose to follow. Meanwhile, others interpret my character by observing those with whom I walk. Well, I want to be like the heroes whom the Old Testament describes as having "walked with God."

Dear Father, give me the determination to walk at Your side. I seek an honorable walk that shows Your power and character. I know that whenever I place myself in Your footsteps, I have victory over the impossible.

UNFAILING PROMISES

"You know in all your hearts and in all your souls that not one thing has failed of all the good things that the LORD your God spoke concerning you. All have come to pass to you, and not one thing of them has failed."
JOSHUA 23:14

Father, You've made so many life-giving promises in Your Word—and every single one of them will come to pass. Many of those promises are made to those who love You and follow You with all their heart. However, I can't make use of those promises if I don't know what they are. Help me to dig deep into Your Word, familiarizing myself with Your promises. I want to know You, God. I want to spend time with You and listen to Your voice. When I get distracted, pull me back to You.

A LIGHT ON MY PATH

Your word is a lamp to my feet
and a light to my path.
PSALM 119:105

Lord, I know what it's like to stumble around in the dark, stubbing my toe, bumping my knees, and knocking things over. Even when my eyes start to adjust, I'm still second-guessing myself because things aren't as clear as they should be. All I can see are shadows and shapes. But You provide a light, Father. When I'm feeling unsure, I ask You to brighten my path so that I don't cause damage as I move along. I praise You, Father, for illuminating the road for me.

INTERNAL CONFLICT

*This I say then: walk in the Spirit, and
you shall not fulfill the lust of the flesh.
For the flesh lusts against the Spirit and
the Spirit against the flesh, and these
are contrary to one another, so that you
cannot do the things that you would.*
GALATIANS 5:16–17

God of power, I thank You for Your Holy
Spirit, who teaches me, encourages me, and
empowers me to battle my fleshly desires.
There's a war raging inside me, and when I
try to overcome temptation through my own
willpower, I fail every time. But when I rely
on Your Holy Spirit, my sinful desires don't
stand a chance. Thank You for making a way
for me to live in accordance with Your will.

JOINED TOGETHER

Now I beseech you, brothers, by the name of our Lord Jesus Christ, that you all speak the same thing and that there be no divisions among you, but that you be perfectly joined together in the same mind and in the same judgment.

1 CORINTHIANS 1:10

This is a hard one, Lord. It's far easier to just hang out with those who agree with me. . .and avoid the ones who don't. But You didn't call me to an easy life. Soften my heart toward those who have a different mindset. Help me love them in spite of our differences. And while You're at it, please soften their hearts too. I long to live at peace with all of my brothers and sisters, bringing joy to Your heart as we walk in unity. Thanks in advance for the work You're going to do, God.

FOR BOLDNESS

*And in nothing terrified by your
adversaries, which is to them an
evident sign of destruction, but to
you of salvation, and that of God.*
Philippians 1:28

Each day, Lord, I encounter people who
have chosen to walk a path contrary to Your
laws and the government's. Their goals defy
honest living, and they think of me as their
adversary. But Father, You give me boldness
greater than my natural ability. I walk by Your
side, and with Your strength, I confront evil
without fearing what others might do to
me. Help me develop strength of spirit and
physical courage. . .and the wisdom to rightly
employ them when needed.

STATEMENT OF PURPOSE

"But none of these things move me. Nor do I count my life dear to myself, so that I might finish my course with joy and the ministry that I have received from the Lord Jesus, to testify to the gospel of the grace of God."
ACTS 20:24

Father, my life is not my own. It's Yours to do with as You please. I know my comfort and rest will come when my work here is done. Any comfort I receive while I'm here is just a bonus, given to me because of Your great love. I should never let these pleasures guide my purpose. This is a hard prayer to say, Lord, and yet I mean every word. I'm Yours. Do with me what You will.

YOU GUIDE ME ALONG

He makes me to lie down in green pastures.
He leads me beside the still waters.
He restores my soul. He leads me in the
paths of righteousness for His name's sake.
Psalm 23:2–3

Father, what a good trailblazer You are! You guide me along all of the right paths which You've chosen just for me. I acknowledge that Your plans are better than my own. I can set my foot on a path, but if it's not the one You designed for me, then it will get me nowhere. So I trust not only in Your guidance, Father, but in Your plan. I can picture Your heavenly blueprints with my name all over them. I submit to the building process, Lord.

KEEPING MY COOL

Therefore, my beloved brothers, let every man be swift to hear, slow to speak, slow to wrath. For the wrath of man does not work the righteousness of God.
JAMES 1:19–20

Father in heaven, I understand that anger itself isn't necessarily sinful, and I know that You call men to speak the truth when necessary. But I also know that if I'm not careful and my understanding is incomplete, I can easily become angry and say things I shouldn't. Please give me a listening ear. Help me hold my tongue when I don't have anything positive to say. I know that my own anger doesn't produce the results You desire, so help me to keep my emotions in check. I want to avoid sinful, damaging anger.

LED BY LOVE

*And walk in love, as Christ has also loved us
and has given Himself for us, an offering and
a sacrifice to God for a sweet-smelling savor.*
EPHESIANS 5:2

I want love to be my guide, Lord. Just as I wouldn't go trekking off into the wilderness without a compass, neither should I try to navigate this life without love. It clears a path better than any machete. When darkness seems to fill the earth, love cuts through brambles, protects from injury, and shines a light on the path ahead. But more than anything, love unifies. It binds me to others—no matter our similarities or differences. Show me how to love as You love, Lord.

A GOOD REPUTATION

Moreover he must have a good report from those who are outside, lest he fall into reproach and the snare of the devil.
1 Timothy 3:7

Father, I carry two names—my own and "Christian." I can't help but notice how difficult it is to restore a reputation once it's been tarnished. So help me develop a good reputation—and keep it. I want Your presence continually in my life so that I can avoid the evil forces that would destroy my name. Only You can soften my character and reset it in the mold You desire. Although I can't live a perfect life, Lord, I know my name will never be tarnished if I follow the guidelines set forth in Your Word.

LIKE AN ANGEL

And looking steadfastly on him,
all who sat in the council saw his face
as if it had been the face of an angel.
ACTS 6:15

God, a man's facial expressions are often a window to his heart. As the people gazed at Stephen, who was about to be stoned for his belief in Christ, his face held a serenity that reminded them of an angel. That makes me wonder: What do others see in me? Frustration? Worry? Fear? Distraction? When people look at me, I want them to see You—Your glory, power, and grace. I want Your presence to be so strong in my life, Lord, that it physically changes my countenance.

NOT IN MYSELF

O Lᴏʀᴅ, I know that the way of man
is not in himself; it is not in man
who walks to direct his steps.
Jᴇʀᴇᴍɪᴀʜ 10:23

The world tells me to look within, Lord. They say that everything I need to know is already inside me. What a foolish notion! The answers aren't found in me. I can plan and devise all I like, but the only true answers are found in You. If I set my own course, I'm sure to land in a ditch. Your directions and plans, however, are perfect. I'll do my best to listen closely as You guide me along a better path.

AN AGREEMENT WITH MY EYES

"I made a covenant with my eyes.
Why then should I think on a maid?"

JOB 31:1

My loving Father in heaven, it's not easy to keep my eyes from seeing things that can cause impure thoughts. I could stop watching television and movies, and I could completely cut myself off from the internet—yet I'd still be bombarded daily with sensual images. Perhaps I should join a monastery? I don't think You want that for me. But like Job, I can start by making an agreement with You—and with my eyes—that I won't intentionally look at anything that could stir up sinful thoughts.

YOUR NAME BRINGS HOPE

And in His name the Gentiles shall trust.
MATTHEW 12:21

Lord, there's so much power in Your name! When the name of Jesus is spoken, demons have to flee. Mountains move. Prayers are answered. Lives are eternally transformed. Your name brings hope—not just to my circumstances and loved ones but to people around the world. That's why the enemy is trying so hard to squelch the name of Jesus—he knows how powerful it is! So I'll go on praising You. . .and watch as miracles unfold. Yours is an awesome, holy name that I'm proud to share with the world.

A SENSE OF WONDER

You are our letter, written in our
hearts, known and read by all men.
2 CORINTHIANS 3:2

Lord, Your Word is a light that guides me to righteousness. It contains moving poetry, stirring songs, thrilling stories of heroes of the faith, and mind-blowing miracles. Each day of reading the Bible is a new adventure.

I pray, Father, that I will always have a sense of wonder when I read Your Word—that it will always stay fresh and illuminate my life. I want to study Your commands, contemplate Your message, and live out its truths throughout each day.

ABOUT FAITH

He did not stagger at the promise of God through unbelief but was strong in faith, giving glory to God and being fully persuaded that He was able also to perform what He had promised. And therefore "it was imputed to him for righteousness."
ROMANS 4:20–22

Father, Abraham had every reason to be anxious. You told him to take his wife and go. . .but You didn't tell him where he was going. You told him his descendants would outnumber the stars. . .yet You didn't give him a son until he was a hundred years old. You promised, and Abraham lived in faith.

You've promised good things to me as well. So forgive me for my doubts. Teach me to live in hope, just like Abraham.

PERFECT PURPOSES

"I know that You can do everything and that no thought can be withheld from You."
JOB 42:2

God, it's remarkable to think that You can do all things. There's not a thing You've ever tried that You didn't accomplish. Me? I try and fail all the time. If You'd put me in charge, I'd ruin everything in a heartbeat. I can't even imagine what it must feel like to have a 100 percent success rate. But because You're the ultimate example of success, I know I can trust You to successfully plan my future—You won't make any mistakes. Today, I'm so grateful that no purpose of Yours can be thwarted.

SERVING ABOVE REPROACH

Avoiding this: that no man should blame us in this abundance that is administered by us, providing for honest things, not only in the sight of the Lord but also in the sight of men.
2 CORINTHIANS 8:20–21

God of righteousness, Your Word tells me that I am to conform my thinking and behavior to the standards You've set for me, not to the world's standards. But at the same time, You want me to make sure my own motives and behaviors never invite scorn or criticism. Lord, You've warned me that the world will oppose me because I serve You. May I never do anything to make it easier for people to criticize.

LOVING ONE ANOTHER

Beloved, if God so loved us, we also
ought to love one another.
1 JOHN 4:11

"Love one another" is such a simple command. But if I'm honest, some people are just tougher to love than others. That's why I want to see people the way You do. I know that Your supernatural love extends to all, even to the most horrible. The man behind bars for that awful crime? You died for him. That woman who abuses her child? You still love her, in spite of her actions. That white-collar boss who defrauded his own workers? You care deeply for him.

I'll never fully understand it, but I want to try. Teach me to love others "in spite of." Then give me ideas for how to show that love—whether to someone in prison or simply to a neighbor who's different than me. I'm excited to learn, Lord.

HONOR

And he said to him, "Behold now, in this city there is a man of God, and he is an honorable man; all that he says surely comes to pass. Now let us go there; perhaps he can show us the way that we should go."

1 Samuel 9:6

Thank You, Lord, for the place of honor You give me in Your kingdom. As armor helps keep a warrior safe in battle, so You shield me from the fiery darts of evil. It's Your assistance that enables me to live a consistently honorable life so that those who don't know You will be drawn to You. To cast off the works of darkness and obtain a good name in my community, I need Your protective covering. My desire is to direct others to heaven.

LIFE AND PEACE

For to be carnally minded is death, but to be spiritually minded is life and peace.

ROMANS 8:6

Father, it's a lot easier to understand something than it is to put it into practice. That's why, despite Your advice in this verse, many of my worries still center around temporary, flesh-and-blood problems. When I center my thoughts on this world, I get stressed out and my quality of life plummets. But when I keep my eyes on You—when I focus my mind on eternity—I have peace in the midst of even the worst situations. Remind me to set my mind on Your Spirit today. I look forward to the life and peace that will follow.

PERSEVERANCE

*For you have need of patience, that
after you have done the will of God,
you might receive the promise.*
HEBREWS 10:36

Lord, I so often reach the point of giving up when I'm following my own path. Somehow, knowing You have the plan gives me the energy to keep pushing forward. I'll endure, Father, submitting myself to Your will, because I know You're ultimately in charge. This isn't always easy, but I'll do my best to put one foot in front of the other on this remarkable path You've carved out for my life.

CONTROLLING THE TONGUE

*If any man among you seems to
be religious and does not bridle his
tongue but deceives his own heart,
this man's religion is worthless.*
JAMES 1:26

Lord God, I sometimes cringe when I read James 1:26. I confess that I occasionally say things that I know are neither pleasing to You or encouraging to others. On my own, it seems that I can't control my tongue any more than I can keep my mind pure or my actions blameless. Forgive me for saying things I shouldn't. Help me speak only words that glorify You and benefit my brothers and sisters in Christ. And when I don't have something good to say, Father, please give me Your good words!

NO BULLYING!

He who walks with wise men shall be wise,
but a companion of fools shall be destroyed.
PROVERBS 13:20

Bullies are terrible, Lord. Whether it's a mean kid on the playground or a manipulative coworker sabotaging a fellow employee, bullies make life miserable for everyone. You know what it feels like to be abused and rejected, Lord. And yet You somehow managed to love the bullies, even when they hung You on a cross. I'll never understand this, but I want to learn from Your example. Help me never to participate in bullying. And help me protect those who are most vulnerable to bullying. I want to make a difference, Lord.

As newborn babies, desire the sincere milk
of the word, that you may grow by it.
1 PETER 2:2

Dear Lord, as a new Christian, I read the Bible to gain spiritual maturity. Unlike my physical body, my spiritual maturity can continue to grow throughout my life. Indeed, reading the Bible provides food for my soul. It helps me grow. But just as importantly, it repairs the damage caused by living in such a spiritually corrosive world each day.

Today, remove the wear and tear on my spiritual body, refashion it, and give it fresh energy through Your renewing Word.

ROLLED BACK

And they said among themselves,
"Who shall roll away the stone from the
door of the sepulchre for us?" And when
they looked, they saw that the stone had
been rolled away, for it was very great.
MARK 16:3–4

Mighty Father, how many times do I worry about a problem. . .only to find You've already taken care of it? When You said to be anxious for nothing, You weren't kidding. You see me at every moment of my life. Not a thing happens to me that You don't already know about. And when boulders block the path You've prepared for me, You've already made arrangements to roll those stones away. I don't have to stress and scheme and figure things out for myself. All I have to do is follow You, trust Your plan, and watch You work miracles in my life.

STRENGTHENED WITH POWER

For this reason I bow my knees to the Father of our Lord Jesus Christ, from whom the whole family in heaven and earth is named, that He would grant you, according to the riches of His glory, to be strengthened with might by His Spirit in the inner man.
EPHESIANS 3:14–16

It's an empowering feeling, Father, to wake up feeling so refreshed and energized that I could take the world by storm. That's what it's like after spending time in Your presence too. Whenever I bring my needs and my concerns to You, I leave feeling much better. You pour out Your Spirit, and Your rushing, supernatural energy fills my veins. I can't drum up this kind of power, Father. It comes only from You. I'm so grateful for Your strength, Lord!

MY SHEPHERD

The LORD is my shepherd. I shall not want.
He makes me to lie down in green pastures.
He leads me beside the still waters. He
restores my soul. He leads me in the paths
of righteousness for His name's sake.

PSALM 23:1–3

Protector God, thank You for being a shepherd to me. A good shepherd guards his sheep and guides them to the best places to eat and rest. Then they can have the energy it takes to face the next day. But You aren't just a *good* shepherd, Lord; You're the *perfect* shepherd. You provide all I need each day, starting with Your love and protection. You restore me when I feel worn down, and You always lead me to a place of righteousness. Thank You, not just for what You do but for who You are.

PREJUDICE

*And do not be conformed to this world,
but be transformed by the renewing of your
mind, that you may prove what is that good
and acceptable and perfect will of God.*
ROMANS 12:2

Some people just don't seem to fit in, Lord. They speak a different language or dress a different way. Their skin color is different. They're from a culture most are not familiar with. As a result, many struggle to find their way in a world that doesn't understand them. Today, please show me how I can combat prejudice anywhere I find it. When You look at us, You don't see people divided by languages and cultures; You see one big happy family. And it's Your will for us to see this too. Show me how I can play a role in making people feel like they fit in.

WORRY

*"Which of you by worrying can
add one cubit to his stature?"*
MATTHEW 6:27

Father, thanks for calming me in times of distress. With Your peace, I smile at my foolish concerns. Some situations are already passed and cannot be changed; others are unlikely to happen; some are trivial and not worth my emotional energy—but worry can make a small concern cast a long shadow. Thankfully, I know You can equip me to deal with the problems I can change. . .and to ignore the ones I can't. I pray that I will see my troubles more clearly with Your wisdom.

THE PRIZE

Do you not know that those who run in a race all run, but one receives the prize? So run, that you may obtain it. And every man who strives for self-control is temperate in all things. Now those do it to obtain a corruptible crown, but we, an incorruptible crown.
1 CORINTHIANS 9:24–25

Dear Father, thank You for this reminder that I need to keep my eye on the prize. Though I won't receive the true prize on this side of eternity, I know the prize is real. It's so much better than those earthly awards and accolades, which provide only temporary thrills. This life is short, and all trophies will end up in a trash heap, abandoned and forgotten. I want the everlasting prize, Father. Help me focus on eternity.

TO PREPARE A PLACE

*"In my Father's house are many mansions;
if it were not so, I would have told you.
I go to prepare a place for you. And if
I go and prepare a place for you, I will
come again and receive you to Myself,
that where I am, there you may be also."*
JOHN 14:2–3

It boggles my mind to think about heaven, Lord. And yet You're already there, preparing a place for me. Your plans for me don't just include the here and now but the hereafter as well. You haven't left anything to chance. Instead, You've breathed new life into my spirit so that I can live out Your plan here on earth and settle into my mansion in heaven once this life is through. What an incredible and generous Savior You are!

A PART TO PLAY

*And He gave some apostles, and some
prophets, and some evangelists, and some
pastors and teachers for the perfecting
of the saints, for the work of the ministry,
for the edifying of the body of Christ.*
EPHESIANS 4:11–12

Lord Jesus, You didn't save me just so that
I could sit in a church pew every Sunday.
Rather, You've given me gifts and abilities so
that I can serve, making a difference in my
congregation and in the world around me.
Here I am, Lord. I want to be an instrument in
Your hand. Move me and enable me to serve
in a way that benefits others and glorifies You.

NO CAUSE TO STUMBLE

Therefore let us not judge one another anymore, but rather judge this: that no man should put a stumbling block or an occasion to fall in his brother's way.

ROMANS 14:13

This is a tough one, Lord! It's easy for me to be critical—to see the flaws in others and not hesitate to point them out. But these words only bring discouragement, especially to folks who are trying hard to do the right thing. I don't want to be the man who causes others to stumble. I long to encourage, not discourage. When I get to heaven, I don't want to see a long line of people who struggled on my account. Instead, I want to see a chain of people who were impacted in a positive way by my kindness and generosity. Help me do better today.

LONG-HAUL ENDURANCE

For this reason I also suffer these things;
nevertheless I am not ashamed, for I
know whom I have believed and am
persuaded that He is able to guard what
I have committed to Him until that day.
2 TIMOTHY 1:12

Lord, whenever my duties and obligations become too much, I sometimes wonder why I must endure them. Yet because of the encouragements in Your Word, I understand that even when I'm beaten down, I am not defeated. Minor problems are opportunities for growth, and they prepare me for the major crises I will surely face along the way.

Prepare me to endure, not just for a moment but for a lifetime.

RESTORE MY SOUL

*The law of the Lᴏʀᴅ is perfect, converting
the soul. The testimony of the Lᴏʀᴅ
is sure, making wise the simple.*
Pꜱᴀʟᴍ 19:7

Dear Father, to restore something means to repair it—to return it to its previous healthy condition. My soul needs restoration. I long to be returned to the way You created mankind to be before sin entered the world. Your Word does that. It makes me more like Christ, which is what You intended me to be in the first place. Your Word grants me the kind of wisdom that surpasses human understanding. I want to dig into Your Word, today and every day. Restore my soul and make me wise.

WALKING OUT YOUR PLAN

I can do all things through Christ
who strengthens me.
PHILIPPIANS 4:13

Because I know Your plans are tailor-made for me, I can rest easy knowing that You'll get me from point A to point B. You know how my feet move. You know how my mind works. You know how my ideas form. There's not a person on the planet who knows me like You do, and there's certainly no one as capable of strengthening my weary bones when I feel like giving up. I submit myself to Your plans, Father. Thank You for the endurance You're giving me today.

SEASONING SALT

*Walk in wisdom toward those who are
without, redeeming the time. Let your
speech always be with grace, seasoned
with salt, that you may know how
you ought to answer every man.*
COLOSSIANS 4:5–6

Lord and Savior, I'm so grateful that You've forgiven me, saved me, and made me a part of Your family of believers. Your Word tells me that I must always be prepared to share Your message of salvation. But I'm just a man, so I don't always know what to say or how to say it. Colossians 4:5–6 suggests that I should tell Your truth in a way that best connects with those I know need You. So may my speech reflect my passion and love for Your message. And please remind me daily why Your gospel is such an amazing message.

RESISTING TEMPTATION

My son, if sinners entice you, do not consent.
PROVERBS 1:10

Temptation is rough, Lord! There have been times I've felt like I was hanging on by my fingertips—unwilling to give in. And on some occasions, I've let go, sliding down into sin. But I don't want to give in. I want to go down kicking and screaming when temptation comes my way. So guard me from relationships that pull me away from You. Even though I want to impact my world—which means sometimes hanging out with people who don't know You yet—I don't ever want to compromise my faith or give up on what I know to be true. Guard my heart and my spirit each day.

DELIGHT

And not only so, but we also rejoice in God through our Lord Jesus Christ, by whom we have now received the atonement.
ROMANS 5:11

All joy comes from You, Lord. I can rejoice because of the risen Christ. I no longer have the heavy weight of my transgressions to discourage me; instead, Your joy lifts my spirit and stamps out my fears. It empowers me to run this spiritual race.

But Lord, for this joy to be fully realized, I must share it with others. My desire is to let this essential fruit of the Spirit flourish in my life. Help me bless others by allowing You to shine through my life.

A CHEERFUL GIVER

*But I say this: he who sows sparingly shall
also reap sparingly, and he who sows
bountifully shall also reap bountifully.
So let every man give as he purposed in
his heart, not grudgingly or of necessity,
for God loves a cheerful giver.*
2 CORINTHIANS 9:6–7

Father, You have given so freely to me. If I
tried to write out all my blessings, I wouldn't
find enough volumes to contain them. Your
generosity is beyond description.

Teach me to find more joy in giving to
others than in receiving for myself. Show
me where You want me to give my time,
resources, and affection, and help me lavish
them freely, even to those who haven't been
generous with me. I want to love relentlessly,
just as You do.

A TAILORED WITNESS

*"But you shall receive power after the
Holy Spirit has come on you, and you
shall be witnesses to Me both in Jerusalem
and in all Judea and in Samaria and
to the farthest part of the earth."*

ACTS 1:8

Where have You called me to go, Lord? How
can I reach others for You? How can I share
Your love, Your plan of salvation, with those
around me? I know You've got specific places
and people in mind—You haven't placed me
here by accident. You've hand-tailored my
surroundings and want me to reach others
in my community for You. Show me, Lord.
Lead. Guide. Empower. I want to be a wit-
ness for You.

FREE TO ACT IN LOVE

*But be careful lest this liberty of yours
by any means becomes a stumbling
block to those who are weak.*

1 Corinthians 8:9

Lord Jesus, thank You for setting me free
from the power of sin and death. No longer
do I have to live in constant worry about what
is right and wrong in Your eyes. Instead, You
let me know when I'm on the right track and
when I need to make changes.

Never let me forget that I must make
my life choices with an eye toward loving
others—especially my brothers in the faith.
I never want to offend someone's conscience or cause someone to slip back into
sinful behavior.

CARING FOR SHUT-INS

Bear one another's burdens,
and so fulfill the law of Christ.
GALATIANS 6:2

Some folks aren't able to tend to their own needs, Lord. They're completely dependent on others. It's hard to imagine what that must feel like. These poor souls may be confined to their homes most of the time. Show me how I can reach out to people in such situations. Should I visit? Offer to clean or pick up a meal? Offer to run errands, sort through medications, or drive them to medical appointments? There's got to be something I can do to help make the days more agreeable. Show me, I pray.

EMERGENCY WORKERS

Defend the poor and fatherless;
do justice to the afflicted and needy.
PSALM 82:3

Almighty God, I pray for those who respond to emergencies—whether police, firefighters, or medical personnel. Please protect these public servants as they come to the rescue of those in dangerous situations. Provide them with the courage and wisdom to extricate victims from the scene of a crisis.

Guide our police as they make split-second decisions in emotionally charged situations. Watch over our firefighters as they rush into harm's way. Give our medical personnel skillful hands and clear minds as they work to save lives. Grant all of these individuals the ability to act quickly and compassionately.

TRANSFORMED

And do not be conformed to this world, but be transformed by the renewing of your mind, that you may prove what is that good and acceptable and perfect will of God.
Romans 12:2

Father, when I read this verse, the words *conform* and *transform* stand out to me. To conform means to comply or take on the shape of something else. To *transform*, however, means to change shape completely. You don't want me to comply with the standards of this world; instead, You want to change me, to make me holy and Christlike. So forgive me for wanting to fit into this world. Transform me into Your image, Father.

MARKED OUT FOR ME

Therefore, since we also are surrounded by such a great a cloud of witnesses, let us lay aside every weight, and the sin that so easily besets us, and let us run with patience the race that is set before us.

HEBREWS 12:1

I can see it now, Lord. I'm at the starting block, just before a big race. A gunshot splits the air and I take off, legs and arms pumping. Except this race is my life, and You have marked it out for me. A turn to the right, a turn to the left—You've left clear signals at the forks in the road. How grateful I am that You took the time to mark my path. As I sprint toward You, I will keep my eye on the prize, Father. With a grateful heart, I run.

LIVING FAITH

What does it profit, my brothers, though a man says he has faith and has not works? Can faith save him? . . . Faith, if it does not have works, is dead, being alone.

JAMES 2:14, 17

Lord Jesus, Your Word says my salvation is a gift from You, granted when I put my faith in Your work on the cross. But You also told Your followers that knowing You would result in good works, all of which glorify You and prove to others that this faith is real and alive. So please show me what good works You want to accomplish today. You've already saved and transformed me, so I want to show my faith to others by the good I do in Your mighty name.

Jesus said to him, "'You shall love the Lord your God with all your heart, and with all your soul, and with all your mind.' This is the first and great commandment. And the second is like it: 'You shall love your neighbor as yourself.' "
MATTHEW 22:37–39

I wonder how things would be, Lord, if I were the one in great need. Would friends and loved ones rush to my aid? Would they provide for every tiny need? I want to tend to those who are struggling in the same way I'd want my own needs to be met. I want to be there so they never forget that someone cares. Show me how to be the best possible friend to people in dire circumstances, Father. Please help me walk with others through their deepest valleys.

LAUGHTER

A merry heart does good like a medicine,
but a broken spirit dries the bones.
PROVERBS 17:22

Heavenly Father, I know You want me to be joyful. . .and the best expression of this joy is laughter. Although there are times to be somber, I realize that reacting to every event with the utmost seriousness can produce a joyless life. May I never present myself with exaggerated dignity. Instead, as a joy-filled man, may I offer an easy smile and an honest laugh that will encourage people to spend time in my presence. I want to always have a joyful outlook that lightens my life and the lives of those around me.

LETTER OF RECOMMENDATION

You are our letter, written in our hearts,
known and read by all men, since you
are manifestly declared to be the letter
of Christ ministered by us, written
not with ink but with the Spirit of the
living God, not on tablets of stone but
on tablets of the human heart.
2 CORINTHIANS 3:2–3

Heavenly Father, what a high compliment! To say that someone's life is Your letter of recommendation is perhaps the highest honor a man of God can obtain. As I read this, I wonder if the same can be said of my own life. I want to live for You. I want my every breath, thought, word, and action to make You proud and reflect Your amazing goodness, mercy, and love. Make me a letter of recommendation, open for all to see.

UNDERSTANDING YOUR WILL

Therefore do not be unwise, but understand what the will of the Lord is.
EPHESIANS 5:17

Lord, I remember how as a child, I didn't always understand the decisions made by the adults in my life. They asked things of me that seemingly made no sense. Now, as an adult myself, I understand that their desires for me were good, not evil. It's the same with You, Father. Though I might not always understand Your will in the moment, everything will be clear at the end. May I always seek to understand Your will, Lord, even when the path appears difficult to navigate.

FORGIVING AS GOD FORGIVES

*Being patient with one another and forgiving
one another if any man has a quarrel against
any. Even as Christ forgave you, so you
also do. And above all these things put on
charity, which is the bond of perfectness.*

COLOSSIANS 3:13–14

Lord Jesus, as You hung on the cross, blood-
ied and bruised from the beatings You'd taken
at the hands of Your executioners, You set an
example for me by saying, "Father, forgive
them, for they do not know what they do"
(Luke 23:34). I have a difficult time understanding that level of forgiveness. It's hard
enough for me to forgive those who have
wronged me in even the smallest ways. But
that's exactly what You tell me to do, Lord.
Please grant me a forgiving heart—just as You
have a forgiving heart toward me.

PRAYING FOR THE WORLD

There is neither Jew nor Greek, there is neither slave nor free, there is neither male nor female. For you are all one in Christ Jesus.
GALATIANS 3:28

Father, this world is filled with billions of people, many of whom have never heard of You. When I observe how (and whom) they worship, I get nervous. Can I ever win them to You when they seem content in their own belief system? Yet Your Word says I'm to preach the gospel to all the world. I don't know how far beyond my own borders I'll ever be able to travel, but one way I can make an impact is by praying. So today, I pray that people of all nations will be won to You, Lord. May the whole earth praise the name of Jesus.

ENCOURAGING THOSE WHO SERVE

*"But charge Joshua and encourage him
and strengthen him, for he shall go over
before this people, and he shall cause them
to inherit the land that you shall see."*

DEUTERONOMY 3:28

Lord, just as Moses encouraged Joshua to lead Your people across the Jordan River to enter the promised land, I want to encourage those who have been chosen to serve. Help me ease their burdens and give them the will to continue the work You have called them to do.

When I am leading others, may I always remember my role as Your servant. Help me to choose the right words and actions to revitalize others when they have grown weary, assure them when they have doubts, console them in times of apparent failure, and reward them with sincere praise for their successes.

SET APART

"Therefore, come out from among them
and be separate," says the Lord. "And
do not touch the unclean thing, and
I will receive you and will be a Father
to you, and you shall be My sons and
daughters," says the Lord Almighty.
2 CORINTHIANS 6:17–18

Holy God, thank You for promising to be a
Father to me, to adopt me fully into Your
family. I am grateful beyond words. Help me
honor the first part of this promise—to be
separate from the world. As Your child, I'm
not supposed to entrench myself in world-
liness. It's sometimes hard to live here but
not really fit in. But I know I fit in perfectly
within Your family. . .and the eternal home
You're preparing for me now. Set me apart
and help me live in a way that honors You.

KNOWN AND SET APART

"Before I formed you in the womb I knew you, and before you came forth out of the womb I sanctified you and ordained you as a prophet to the nations."

JEREMIAH 1:5

What a stunning revelation, God, to know that not only did You watch out for me in the womb, but You called me, chose me, and sanctified me—set me apart—even as my bones were forming! How perfect are Your plans for my life, Father, that You took the time to set them in motion before I even drew my first breath. You are truly astounding, Lord!

OUR SOURCE OF WISDOM

*If any of you lacks wisdom, let him ask of
God, who gives to all men generously and
without reproach, and it shall be given him.
But let him ask in faith, without wavering.
For he who wavers is like a wave of the
sea driven and tossed with the wind.*

JAMES 1:5–6

Each day, Lord, I face situations that require
me to act wisely. So today, please give me
the wisdom to choose words and actions that
glorify You and benefit others. I know You've
promised to give me wisdom when I ask for
it—and I trust this promise wholeheartedly.
I will leave the "how" up to You.

WORTHY OF YOUR CALLING

*Therefore also we pray always for you
that our God will count you worthy of this
calling and fulfill all the good pleasure of His
goodness and the work of faith with power.*
2 Thessalonians 1:11

I sense it, Father—You have big plans for me on the horizon. Sometimes, I wonder how I'll find the time or energy for it all. . .but then I'm reminded of all You've brought me through already. I know that with Your help, I can do anything. Today, I commit myself to pray over the things I can't see yet. Prayer will activate my faith and empower me to step out when the time comes. This kind of power can only be birthed on my knees.

May my life be worthy of the call.

GRACE

Therefore, since we are receiving a kingdom that cannot be moved, let us have grace, by which we may serve God acceptably with reverence and godly fear.
HEBREWS 12:28

Father, I know I'll never obtain perfection in this life. That's why I'm so grateful for Your generous grace and mercy. I know Your forgiveness is without limits, provided I show the same forgiveness to others. So my prayer is twofold: Please bless my undertakings and wrap them in Your clemency so that even when I fail, I will remain under Your protection. And please send Your Holy Spirit to help me forgive repeatedly without harboring resentment.

SEE AND LOVE

Then, looking at him, Jesus loved him and said to him, "One thing you lack: go your way, sell whatever you have, and give to the poor, and you shall have treasure in heaven. And come, take up the cross and follow Me."
MARK 10:21

Lord Jesus, these are tough words You spoke to the rich young ruler. But perhaps equally challenging is the attitude with which You spoke them. As You looked at the man, You *loved* him. You didn't judge him. You spoke with sincerity of heart, wanting only the best for him.

When I look at others, do I love them? Do I truly see people who desperately need You? Forgive me for failing to view others as You do. Give me Your heart, Father. Help me truly see and love those You place in my path.

BOLD PROCLAMATIONS

*But you are a chosen generation, a royal
priesthood, a holy nation, a special
people, that you should declare the
praises of Him who has called you out
of darkness into His marvelous light.*
1 PETER 2:9

I'll proclaim it, Lord—You are a most excellent
Father, worthy of praise! Grow my boldness,
that I might tell others that there is a God
who can pull them out of dark places and into
marvelous light. If I don't find the courage to
share this good news, who will? You've called
me and set me apart for this very purpose.
So today, I will tell others how mighty You
are. Thank You for making me a hope-giver,
Father. I want to be like You.

WORTHWHILE SUFFERING

For to you it is given on behalf of
Christ, not only to believe in Him,
but also to suffer for His sake.
PHILIPPIANS 1:29

Lord, I hate the idea of suffering. But my love for You and for others makes me willing to do just that if necessary. I know I'll probably never be burned at the stake or tossed to the lions. But if my twenty-first-century rights and privileges ever come under fire because of my faith, help me to see it as a gift. May I continue trusting in You so that I can push through these difficulties in a way that helps others see Your glory.

HEART, SOUL, AND MIND

*Trust in the LORD with all your heart and
do not lean on your own understanding.
In all your ways acknowledge Him,
and He shall direct your paths.*

PROVERBS 3:5–6

Loving You, Lord, is more than a feeling. It means realigning my heart, soul, mind, hopes, and dreams with Your plan. It means serving You with my aspirations and tomorrows. It means trusting that You're for me, not against me. It means believing You hold the answer to any trial I might face.

Only in loving You will I find comfort, peace, and solutions. There is none like You, Father, and I am grateful to be Your child.

*"His glory covered the heavens,
and the earth was full of His praise."*

HABAKKUK 3:3

Almighty Father of all creation, accept this prayer of praise. I respect You, venerate You, and honor You as the Creator of the universe and everything it holds. I recognize You as my Maker. I am thankful that You were too kind to walk away from the world You made. Instead, You take an interest in my daily life and care about my eternal well-being.

I know I'll never understand enough of Your power to fully appreciate it. . .but that will not stop me from trying. May I always praise You for Your love, Jesus' grace, and the Holy Spirit's guidance.

HAVE FAITH

And Jesus answered and said to him,
"What do you want Me to do for you?"
The blind man said to Him, "Lord, that I
might receive my sight." And Jesus said to
him, "Go your way. Your faith has made
you well." And immediately he received
his sight and followed Jesus on the road.
MARK 10:51–52

Father, this man's sight was restored because of his faith. And Your Word is filled with proof that You reward our sincere belief. You may not always act in the way I want You to, but I'll stay confident in Your love and strength.

I believe You are God. I believe in Your ultimate power and Your overwhelming grace. Give me the faith of this blind man. I believe.

YOU SPEAK TO ME

*"Have I not commanded you? Be strong
and of good courage. Do not be afraid
or be dismayed, for the LORD your
God is with you wherever you go."*

JOSHUA 1:9

It's an age-old question, Lord: How can I hear
Your voice? Is it really still and small, or do
Your words shake the earth? Can I hear You
in the stillness of a forest or in the cries of
a newborn? Will I find Your thoughts in the
Bible? Your laws carved on my heart?

The truth is, I can hear only if my spiritual ears are opened, so I offer them to You
today. Speak, Lord, in any way You choose.
Bolster my courage with Your empowering
voice. I'm listening, Father. Ears wide open.

WHEN I SIN

My little children, I write these things to you, that you may not sin. And if any man sins, we have an advocate with the Father, Jesus Christ the righteous. And He is the propitiation for our sins, and not for ours only, but also for the sins of the whole world.
1 John 2:1–2

God of grace and forgiveness, thank You for sending Jesus, Your only Son, to earth so that I can be forgiven for my sins. You have transformed my thinking and behavior, but I still do things that don't please or glorify You. Thank You, Jesus, for pleading my case before the Father. Thank You for making me righteous in Your eyes, even after I blow it. And when I do sin, may I confess it and turn away from it quickly.

UNTIL THAT DAY

*And this I pray that. . .you may be
sincere and without offense until the
day of Christ, being filled with the fruits
of righteousness, which are by Jesus
Christ, to the glory and praise of God.*
PHILIPPIANS 1:9–11

Lord, You're showing me day by day how
to make better choices, and I'm grateful
for the growth I see in my spiritual life. I'm
finally figuring out how to say no to the bad
stuff and yes to the good. I want more than
anything to please You. People know I'm a
Christian, and I know they're curious to see
if I'm actually as dedicated as I say I am. I
want to be authentic, the real deal. You've
cleansed me with Your blood, so may I live a
life worthy of that cleansing—one filled with
good deeds that bring glory to Your name.

STAYING CONNECTED

*And He is the head of the body,
the church, who is the beginning, the
firstborn from the dead, that in all things
He might have the preeminence.*
COLOSSIANS 1:18

I feel more connected to You, Jesus, when I meet with other believers. The house of God provides a plot of fertile soil where my knowledge of You can grow and my soul can find refreshment. Each time I attend church, I acknowledge You as my Savior. It is one way I demonstrate to others my commitment to You.

Lord, I pray I will always look to You as the head of the church.

*"Watch therefore, for you know
neither the day nor the hour in which
the Son of Man is coming."*
MATTHEW 25:13

Lord Jesus, I know You said we won't know the day or hour of Your return. But You did give us signs to watch for. . .and it sure seems like You're coming soon. Help me to live as if each moment could be my last chance to please You. Pour out Your grace and power through my life. With everyone I meet, may I be a beacon of Your compassion and generosity. I know Your love draws others to You, so help me love like You do, with reckless abandon. On the day You arrive to take Your people home, I want to be ready—no regrets.

YOU NEVER LIE

"God is not a man, that He should lie, nor the son of man, that He should repent. Has He said, and shall He not do it? Or has He spoken, and shall He not make it good?"
NUMBERS 23:19

Your Word is always truthful, Lord. I can trust that what You say will be fulfilled. You're not like the people I've known who say one thing but mean another. Sometimes, people—myself included—have great intentions when they make promises. . .but they don't follow through. Some say, "Sure, I'll be there for you," and then they're not. But You're not like that, Father. Every promise You've ever spoken is solid-gold truth. I'm so grateful.

A LIFE OF INTEGRITY

He who walks uprightly walks surely, but he who perverts his ways shall be known.

PROVERBS 10:9

Lord Jesus, during Your time here on earth, You were the perfect example of integrity. You never compromised when it came to following Your Father's law, and You never wavered in doing what He had sent You to do. I want to live that kind of life. I want You and the rest of the family to see me as a man of integrity—as a man changed by his adoption into Your family. May I always follow Your Word first and never compromise on what You tell me is right. Help me to love and obey You with a pure heart and with an eye toward Your eternal kingdom.

THE NARROW GATE

"Enter in at the narrow gate, for wide is the gate and broad is the way that leads to destruction, and there are many who go in by it. Because the gate is narrow and the way is narrow that leads to life, and there are few who find it."

MATTHEW 7:13–14

The gospel message flies in the face of political correctness, Lord. It's getting to the point where standing up for You often draws accusations of bigotry and hate. Neither of those words apply to me! I love all people. But it's still true that there's only one way to heaven—through Your Son, Jesus Christ. So I'll go on proclaiming that life-changing message, no matter how difficult. Help me as I speak up today.

DELIVERANCE FROM CAPTURE

*And this I pray. . .that you may approve
things that are excellent, that you may
be sincere and without offense until the
day of Christ, being filled with the fruits
of righteousness, which are by Jesus
Christ, to the glory and praise of God.*
PHILIPPIANS 1:9–11

Heavenly Father, I know that Satan is like a spider, forever spinning webs to snare wandering victims. Some of these traps are in obscure places, but they are tailor-made for each man's particular weakness.

Lord, guard my mind, spirit, and body from Satan's lures. Deliver me when I'm tempted to violate Your laws. Only with Your help can I maintain a holy lifestyle and avoid Satan's deception.

THE GREAT COMMISSION

"Therefore go and teach all nations, baptizing them in the name of the Father and of the Son and of the Holy Spirit, teaching them to observe all the things that I have commanded you. And behold, I am with you always, even to the end of the world."

MATTHEW 28:19–20

Dear Father, as I read this passage—which some call the Great Commission—I wonder how well I'm stacking up. Am I making disciples? Am I teaching others to observe all Your commandments? Am I actively leading people to You?

I know You've promised to be right beside me through every moment—to never leave me, even when I face rejection from others. So help me fulfill my part in this commission as I share Your love with those around me. Give me courage and fortitude as I live out this commandment.

I DECLARE!

*If you confess with your mouth the Lord
Jesus and believe in your heart that
God has raised Him from the dead, you
shall be saved. For with the heart man
believes to righteousness, and with the
mouth confession is made to salvation.*

Romans 10:9–10

Lord, Your declarations are powerful. But
You're teaching me that mine can be too.
Today, I openly declare that Jesus Christ is
Lord. I choose to believe that You raised Him
from the dead, Father. And because I truly
believe what I'm declaring, I know I'm made
right with You. This amazing declaration has
truly changed my life—and my eternity. All
praise belongs to You!

BECAUSE OF YOUR MERCY

Not by works of righteousness that we have done, but according to His mercy He saved us, by the washing of regeneration and renewing of the Holy Spirit.

TITUS 3:5

Almighty Savior, thank You for bringing me into Your eternal kingdom and transforming me through the power of Your love and Your Holy Spirit. I know You want me to do good works for Your kingdom and for other people. But those things happen as a *result* of my salvation, not the *reason* for it. There's nothing I do on my own to escape the consequences of my sin. You've done it all, renewing me by Your Holy Spirit. Humble me and help me focus on the fact that I'm saved only because of Your mercy.

PRAYING FOR MY FRIENDS

And the LORD turned the captivity of Job when he prayed for his friends. Also the LORD gave Job twice as much as he had before.
JOB 42:10

There are so many lessons to be learned from Job's story, Lord, but here's one that's easy to overlook: You waited to restore Job's fortune until after he had prayed for his friends. Sometimes, I wonder why You're taking so long to move on my behalf. Maybe You're just waiting on me to lift up a prayer for someone!

I want to be a man who prays for others— not just during rough seasons but on a regular basis. Thanks for the reminder that praying for them is both a blessing and an honor.

BEING WITH BELIEVERS

I was glad when they said to me,
*"Let us go into the house of the L*ORD*."*
PSALM 122:1

Reading the Bible, talking to You in prayer, singing hymns, and meeting with other Christians inspire me to a closer walk with You, heavenly Father. I need to assemble with other Christians because I gain strength by associating with those who love You. These actions help fortify my spiritual life—and only by becoming strong in You can I plow through obstacles.

But Lord, just as I need the fellowship of dedicated believers, help me realize that they need me too. Each of us are blessed through fellowship with one another.

DIPLOMACY

*Then Paul stood in the middle of Mars' Hill
and said: "Men of Athens, I perceive that
in all things you are too superstitious. . . .
God, who made the world and all things in it,
seeing that He is Lord of heaven and earth,
does not dwell in temples made with hands.
Nor is He worshipped with men's hands."*
ACTS 17:22, 24–25

Father, when Paul was addressing the Greeks, he didn't charge in like a bull, calling them pagans and insulting their beliefs. He began with a statement of respect. He used tact and diplomacy, and his approach earned him their listening ears. Many Greeks left their pagan ways to follow You, but they may not have if Paul had been rude or overbearing. Teach me to use tact and diplomacy in my conversations with others so that they'll be open to hearing about You.

AN ETERNAL PERSPECTIVE

Then Peter said, "I have no silver and gold, but I give you such as I have: In the name of Jesus Christ of Nazareth, rise up and walk!"
ACTS 3:6

When people hear the word *prosper*, their thoughts often shift to money, big houses, and fancy cars. But You are changing our thinking about this word, Lord. You're giving us an eternal perspective. We can't take money with us when we die. So instead of focusing on those things, I ask that You give me an eternal perspective today. I may be short on silver and gold, but I do have a heavenly outlook that is giving me courage to walk into tomorrow with confidence. Thank You, Father!

RESPONDING TO POWER

Now when Daniel knew that the writing was signed, he went to his house, and—his windows being open in his room toward Jerusalem—he knelt on his knees three times a day and prayed and gave thanks before his God, as he did formerly.

DANIEL 6:10

Lord, I sometimes feel shocked at my culture's lack of concern for You and Your standards. I'm grieved when I see how people conduct themselves today. But I don't want these things to bring me to a point of anger or fear. Instead, may they bring me to my knees in prayer. May I continually pray for this culture, my political leaders, and those who I know desperately need Your touch.

MEETING TOGETHER

And let us consider one another to provoke to love and to good works, not forsaking the assembling of ourselves together, as is the manner of some, but exhorting one another, and so much the more as you see the Day approaching.
HEBREWS 10:24–25

Some Sundays, I just don't feel like getting out of bed. But You've shown me time and time again how different my day can be when I go to church—even when I don't feel like it. So continue nudging me, Lord. Don't let me slip into laziness or apathy. Keep me yearning for time with You and my fellow believers. I want to go on provoking others to good works, and that can only happen when we're actually together. This is more important now than ever, since the day of Christ's return is drawing closer. Bind us together, Lord, I pray.

WORTHY OF HONOR

*O LORD our Lord, how excellent is
Your name in all the earth!*
PSALM 8:9

Majestic Lord, I've seen microscopic pictures of a single snowflake, and I've seen images of stars and galaxies uncountable. When I observe the grandeur of Your vast creation, I'm brought to my knees in wonder, consumed by a single question: Why would an all-powerful God like You concern Yourself with my life?

I may never know. All I know is that when I'm apprehensive, I can trust You to keep me safe. When I'm alone, You speak to me. When I'm down, You make me glad. When I'm weak, I bow before You and feel Your strength.

SUN AND SHIELD

For the Lord God is a sun and shield.
The Lord will give grace and glory;
no good thing will He withhold
from those who walk uprightly.
PSALM 84:11

All-sufficient Father, You are my sun, giving light to my path. You are my shield, protecting me in ways I may not even realize. You pour out Your grace on my life. As I look back, I can see You've never withheld anything I've needed. I want to walk as a man of integrity—a sincere reflection of Your glory, kindness, and love. Give me a heart for justice, mercy, and compassion, and grant me humility as I deal with others. I love You, Father, and praise You for Your goodness.

PURE TRUTH

A wise man will hear and will increase learning, and a man of understanding shall attain wise counsels.

Proverbs 1:5

Lord, the world is filled with counselors. . .but much of the advice that is touted today is far removed from the teachings found in Your Word. All I have to do is go online or walk outdoors to find horrible counsel. And while it's easy to spot error most of the time, it gets harder when the enemy starts using the language of truth to communicate his lies. That's why this verse says wisdom is so important—only by learning Your pure truth and taking it to heart can I realize whenever someone is trying to pervert it. Help me today in my quest to learn more about You.

HANDLING REGRETS

"And I will restore to you the years that the locust has eaten, the cankerworm, and the caterpillar, and the palmerworm, My great army that I sent among you."

JOEL 2:25

Forgiving God, there are things in my past I'm not proud of—things that make me cringe upon remembrance. If I could go back and do some things differently, I would. But You, Lord, have promised me that You're using everything, even those bad decisions, for my good and for Your glory. There's nothing I can do to change the past, but there's plenty You can do to teach me important lessons and give me wisdom to impart to others. Lord, continually remind me that You are the perfect Redeemer—even when it comes to my past.

BY ONE SPIRIT

For by one Spirit we were all baptized into one body, whether we are Jews or Gentiles, whether we are slaves or free, and all were made to drink into one Spirit.

1 CORINTHIANS 12:13

There's so much disunity in the world today, Lord. It's almost like people are working overtime to put up walls of separation. May that never be the case inside the body of Christ. We are, after all, baptized by the same Holy Spirit. No matter where we came from— no matter our color or heritage—all true Christians are one in You. You've unified us, stitched us together into a colorful quilt known as the body of Christ. So may our differences never separate us, Lord. May they only draw us closer.

A SPECIAL PLANET

He loves righteousness and judgment.
The earth is full of the goodness of the LORD.
PSALM 33:5

Heavenly Father, photos of earth taken from space are stunning in the beauty they reveal: green forests, brown deserts, blue-green oceans, and white clouds. The earth looks like a marvelous jewel set in an infinite sea of black. It—and all the smaller marvels found within—causes me to worship You, Lord, and remember You as the Creator.

But help me always be mindful that this earth is not my permanent home. Despite its beauty, the earth is but a way station to a much grander place with You. May I always live my life with the knowledge that heaven is my eventual destination.

LET THEM SEE YOU

*But they had heard only that he who
persecuted us in times past now preached
the faith that once he destroyed,
and they glorified God in me.*
GALATIANS 1:23–24

Good Father, do others glorify You because
of me? When they look at my life, do they
see the miracle of Your presence? Do they
see Your influence in my actions and atti-
tudes? I hope so. It's easy for my words and
deeds to turn people away from You. May
that never happen, Lord. Make my life such
a clear reflection of Your love that others
see You instead of me. I want to be a mirror
of Your kindness and grace to those around
me. Let them see all the marvelous things
You've done in my life. Let them see You.

FOR MY SAKE

But He was wounded for our transgressions,
He was bruised for our iniquities. The
chastisement of our peace was on Him,
and with His lashes we are healed.
Isaiah 53:5

If I needed any additional proof that You want the best for me, Father, I need look no further than Your Son. How sobering it is to realize that He took the punishment for my sins. I deserved to be punished. . .but received only good instead. You owed me nothing. . .but You gave me everything. When I put this in perspective, Father, I realize that I should be doing everything for Your sake. Today, I commit myself to trying harder. May I focus more on Your will than my own, Lord.

A PERFECT EXAMPLE

"But whoever wants to be great among you shall be your minister, and whoever of you wants to be the first shall be servant of all. For even the Son of Man did not come to be ministered to, but to minister, and to give His life as a ransom for many."
MARK 10:43–45

Lord Jesus, You are the perfect example of a godly servant. You came to earth to teach, preach, and rebuke those You knew were wrong. But more than that, You came to serve—even to the point of giving up Your very life so that others could live forever. I know, Jesus, that You want me to do great works for You. Let those things flow from my willingness to serve others first, just like You did.

ALL THINGS

*And He has put all things under His feet
and gave Him to be the head over all
things to the church, which is His body,
the fullness of Him who fills all in all.*
Ephesians 1:22–23

Lord, Your Word clearly says that all things
are placed under the feet of Your Son, Jesus.
Consequently, I can put all things under His
control—my thoughts, motives, mistakes,
hurts, and sicknesses. He cares about it all
and bids me to take refuge in Him. Today, I
choose to do just that. I won't wait until I'm
sitting in church on Sunday morning. Right
here, right now, I'll give Him my struggles
and regrets. Take them, I pray, and release
me from their burden. I'm so grateful I can
trust You in *all* things, Lord.

RIGHTEOUSNESS

And the LORD said to Noah, "You and all your house come into the ark, for I have seen you righteous before Me in this generation."

GENESIS 7:1

Lord, when I see sin running wild in this world, it's sometimes tempting to let my guard down and say or do something I know is wrong. In moments like that, remind me of Noah's story. He refused to compromise his righteous walk with You, Lord. The evil people of his day mocked him as he built the ark, but You honored his righteousness by saving him and his family from the flood.

Dear God, help me find favor in Your eyes by being a man of Christian values. My utmost concern is to please You.

SEEK GOOD

*Seek good, and not evil, that you may live.
And so the LORD, the God of hosts, shall be
with you, as you have spoken. Hate evil,
love good, and establish judgment in the
gate. It may be that the LORD God of hosts
will be gracious to the remnant of Joseph.*

AMOS 5:14–15

Dear Father, I know You are good, and I know You reward goodness in Your people. I was created in Your image, but Satan wants to deform that image. He wants to draw me into evil thoughts, filling my mind with pettiness, anger, and envy. Help me fight him off, Father! I want to be holy like You. I want my thoughts, words, and actions to reflect Your character as I honor You with everything I do.

YOU BRING ME FORTH AS GOLD

"But He knows the way that I take. When He has tested me, I shall come forth as gold."
JOB 23:10

Lord, the phrase *trial by fire* is frightening indeed. Going through the fire is never fun. . .but the results are astounding. Trials purify me and rid me of the things that drag me down. Your plans for me are so holy, Lord, that they require me to be the best I can be. So cleanse my heart today, Father. Burn away my imperfections and shape me into Your image. Bring me from the furnace, a new man of God, ready to do Your will. I submit myself to the process, Lord.

THE OBJECT OF MY LOVE

If any man loves the world, the love of the Father is not in him. For all that is in the world—the lust of the flesh, and the lust of the eyes, and the pride of life—is not of the Father but is of the world.

1 JOHN 2:15–16

Lord Jesus, You once told Your followers that no one can serve two masters—one will always pull our love and attention away from the other. Your Word tells me I can't love You and the world at the same time. I have to live in this world, but I know I can't love its ways. May my love be focused on You alone so that my heart is never divided. I don't want to be tempted to serve anything but You.

THE HOUSEHOLD OF FAITH

Therefore, as we have opportunity, let us do good to all men, especially to those who are of the household of faith.

GALATIANS 6:10

I know we're called to treat all people with love and respect, Lord, but I'm glad You gave us a little nudge to be especially good to those in the body of Christ. I have such admiration for my spiritual brothers and sisters. Many have lived difficult lives, but they've persevered for the sake of the gospel. Show me how to bring honor to the ones who've been so good to me and my family. I want to bless them for their years of service and love. Give me fresh and creative ideas so that I can bring honor where honor is due, Lord.

ON THE FRONT LINE

And how shall they preach unless they are sent? As it is written, "How beautiful are the feet of those who preach the gospel of peace and bring glad tidings of good things!"
ROMANS 10:15

Good Shepherd, I pray for the missionaries who teach the gospel at the risk of their own lives. I deeply respect and support those brave individuals who are willing to follow that calling. May their words and deeds radiate the gospel to the destitute, sick, suffering, and spiritually barren.

And Lord, may their example encourage me to support those who step out in faith so that they will be fully equipped to effectively spread the gospel to the world. Energize them and protect them from those who resent their efforts.

EVERLASTING COVENANT

"And I will make an everlasting covenant with them, that I will not turn away from them to do them good, but I will put My fear in their hearts, that they shall not depart from Me."

JEREMIAH 32:40

Dear Father, Your promises aren't like man's promises. When a person makes a promise, circumstances may prevent its fulfillment. But Your covenant is certain and unchanging. You promised to never turn away from me, because I am Your child. You promised to bless me every day of my life. Even when I run from You, fleeing Your presence, Your love chases me. Forgive me for running, Lord. Today and every day, place a holy reverence for You in my heart and draw me nearer to You.

YOU KNOW MY PATH

When my spirit was overwhelmed within me,
then You knew my path. In the way where I
walked they have secretly laid a snare for me.
PSALM 142:3

Lord, I know that not everyone is for me. Some would rather see me fail. . .and they may even try to knock me off my path. But I won't let them get me down or send me veering in the wrong direction. Even when they weaken my resistance, I'll keep my focus on You. You're the only one who knows the direction this road is leading. How could I *not* trust You? No matter how many traps are set, You'll guide me safely past them so that I can continue to grow in You. I praise You for that, Lord.

A MATTER OF TRUST

*Trust in the LORD with all your heart and
do not lean on your own understanding.
In all your ways acknowledge Him,
and He shall direct your paths.*

PROVERBS 3:5–6

God, it's not always easy for me to trust another person completely, because even the best people I know sometimes fall short. But not You. I'm thankful, Lord, that I can always count on You. You have proven Yourself trustworthy, not just in the lives of all the saints before me but in my own life as well. Help me to always remember Your trustworthiness, especially when I need encouragement, comfort, or direction. Help me look beyond my own circumstances and trust You fully to guide and direct me.

THROUGH FAITH, WE UNDERSTAND

Through faith we understand that the worlds were formed by the word of God, so that things that are seen were not made of things that appear.

HEBREWS 11:3

There are things I'll never understand, Lord—how a saint can fall to temptation, how a parent can abuse a child, how a person can turn away from You and return to a life of sin. But You're dropping the blinders from my eyes, giving me glimpses of the spiritual world. I notice when the enemy is at work, toying with believers. With eyes of faith, I understand that dark and drastic leaps begin with small steps. I also see that it's more important than ever to stick close to You and to ask for Your perspective on things. These are precarious times, Lord. Thank You for letting me see what's really going on out there.

Do not let any man despise your youth, but be an example to the believers in word, in conversation, in love, in spirit, in faith, in purity.
1 TIMOTHY 4:12

Heavenly Father, I never want to become a deceiver who tries to live two lives. For if I live two lives, one of them must die. Good cannot exist at the same time as deception. I pray that it's the false, hypocritical me that bites the bullet. Although I can't achieve the sinless life of Christ, help me to follow Your Word so closely that I illustrate a true Christian life. I pray that my example is not a grainy copy but a perfect replica—born in Your likeness, educated in Your love, and reflecting Your grandeur.

THE SHIELD

Above all, taking the shield of faith,
with which you shall be able to quench
all the fiery darts of the wicked.
EPHESIANS 6:16

My enemy is powerful, Father, and he has some pretty nasty weapons. To engage him in battle without the proper armor would be foolish. I'd be just asking for flaming arrows to pierce my soul. I couldn't possibly win such a battle. But You've provided the very best protection: faith. I can wield my faith like a shield against all sorts of attacks, and those arrows will immediately fall to the ground. Build my faith, Father, as a strong shield against life's cruel assaults. Make me a strong warrior.

MY THOUGHT LIFE MATTERS

Finally, brothers, whatever things are true, whatever things are honest, whatever things are just, whatever things are pure, whatever things are lovely, whatever things are of good report, if there is any virtue, and if there is any praise, think on these things.

PHILIPPIANS 4:8

When my hope is waning, remind me of this verse, Lord. My thoughts always lead to actions (good or bad), so keep my thoughts on the things that please You. I want to focus on Your truth, not on the deceptions of this world. I need to dwell on noble things—like caring for the poor and tending to those in need. Help me shift my thoughts to doing good and remaining pure (a task that isn't always easy in today's society). Lord, may I reflect You to a watching world.

AMAZING POWER AND LOVE

"Ah, Lord GOD! Behold, You have made the heavens and the earth by Your great power and outstretched arm, and there is nothing too hard for You."
JEREMIAH 32:17

Lord God, as a mere man, my power is severely limited. I can't change people's hearts, I can't control world events, I can't revive the dead, and I *certainly* can't rescue anyone from the consequences of sin. But You can. You are my Creator—the Creator of the whole universe—and there is nothing You can't do. I can't fully comprehend Your incredible power. I stand amazed that a God of such might actually cares for such an insignificant creature as me. Thank You for being big and powerful enough to create all I see, yet kind and loving enough to reach down to me individually.

IMMEASURABLY MORE

Now to Him who is able to do exceedingly abundantly above all that we ask or think, according to the power that works in us, to Him be glory in the church by Christ Jesus throughout all ages, world without end. Amen.
EPHESIANS 3:20–21

You are an "above and beyond" Father. You don't just give Your children what they need or what they ask for. You give us immeasurably more. And it's all by Your power, not ours. What a relief!

Today, may the blessings You've lavished on me show Your glory—in both the church and the world. For generations, may people share of the great things You've done. I'm so grateful for the work You're doing in my life.

EYES FORWARD

I will lift up my eyes to the hills. Where does my help come from? My help comes from the Lord, who made heaven and earth.
PSALM 121:1–2

Sometimes, Father, I get distracted by events that take place around me. And other times, my prayers are laced with concerns. But when I turn my eyes toward You, I can see that the trials of this life are well worth the destination. Build in me the assurance that You care about the matters I bring before You—and that peace is only a prayer away. Thank You for listening to my appeal.

CONFIDENCE

Therefore do not cast away your confidence, which has great recompense of reward. For you have need of patience, that after you have done the will of God, you might receive the promise.
HEBREWS 10:35–36

Unchanging Father, these verses were written to the Hebrew Christians, who'd been ridiculed and abused for their faith. They'd suffered greatly for associating with the name of Christ. . .but they'd also endured with confidence. Yet after they'd been through so much, some of them still wanted to turn back!

I haven't been through anything close to what those early believers endured, but it's sometimes tempting to lose faith. I want to stay the course, to endure, to cling to my confidence and faith. Give me the raw strength I need to endure to the end, Father.

SURE OF WHAT I HOPE FOR

"Blessed is the man who trusts in the
LORD, and whose hope is the LORD."
JEREMIAH 17:7

Confident. Sure. These words propel me,
Father. I want to remain confident, even
during the rough seasons. I want to square my
shoulders, stare my problems in the eye, and
know for certain that You're going to come
through for me. This takes faith, I know, but
You are the author of faith. So that's what I
ask for today, Lord. Give me faith to believe
for assurance—to stand strong when others
around me are falling. May I be sure of what
I hope for, God.

A BOOK I CAN TRUST

*Knowing this first, that no prophecy of
scripture is of any private interpretation. For
the prophecy did not come in old time by
the will of man, but holy men of God spoke
as they were moved by the Holy Spirit.*
2 PETER 1:20–21

Thank You, God, for going to such amazing lengths to give me the Bible. I know I can trust Your written Word because Your own Holy Spirit inspired men of Your own choosing to write it. Its words reflect Your heart, relaying every promise, command, and bit of wisdom I need to live a faithful life that pleases You. I confess that I sometimes don't read Your Word as regularly as I should. Help me make time in Your Word a daily priority.

COMPASSION FOR LOCAL MISSIONS

And be kind to one another, tenderhearted,
forgiving one another, even as God
for Christ's sake has forgiven you.
EPHESIANS 4:32

Sometimes, I simply forget, Lord, that there are hurting people all around me: from children at the local cancer hospital to elderly people who are unable to leave their homes to parents caring for special needs kids. Soup kitchens need cooks. Single moms need their cars fixed. So today, God, increase my compassion. Give me a heart for a local ministry and then show me how best to give. I'm getting excited just thinking about the possibilities! Thanks for using me, Lord.

And God said, "Behold, I have given you every herb-bearing seed that is on the face of all the earth and every tree, in which is the fruit of a tree-yielding seed; to you it shall be for food."

GENESIS 1:29

I praise You, Living God, who made all things. You spoke into existence the plant and animal kingdoms. You created humanity in Your image to care for Your creation.

Thank You, Lord, for the fruitful seasons that are made possible by Your design—the seasons of seedtime and harvest. I see eternity in the seeds of each fruit and vegetable because they ensure a harvest year after year. For the blessings of the dinner table, whether a simple staple like bread or a hearty main course, I give You praise, O Lord.

YOU WILL FIGHT FOR ME

"Be strong and courageous. Do not be afraid or dismayed because of the king of Assyria or because of all the multitude that is with him, for there are more with us than with him. With him is an arm of flesh, but with us is the LORD our God to help us and to fight our battles." And the people trusted the words of Hezekiah, king of Judah.
2 CHRONICLES 32:7–8

Dear Father, since the beginning of time, You've told Your people to be strong and courageous. In this passage, the people didn't need to fear the king of Assyria. He was strong. . .but You were stronger. In the same way, I don't need to fear the circumstances that threaten my peace, joy, and well-being. I know You will fight my battles for me. Thank You, Father. I trust You completely.

UP FROM THE GRAVE

Who through Him believe in God, who raised
Him up from the dead and gave Him glory,
that your faith and hope might be in God.
1 PETER 1:21

Hope is not some lifeless thing, Lord. It's living and breathing and coursing through my veins even now. Hope boosts my adrenaline. Hope steadies my breathing. Hope shifts my focus. Hope keeps my feet moving. And this amazing hope is fueled by the resurrection of Your Son, Jesus. When He rose from the dead, He created a hope that refuses to die. What a staggering gift of motivation, Father. I praise You for this hope.

GOOD AND PERFECT GIFTS

*Every good gift and every perfect gift
is from above and comes down from
the Father of lights, with whom there
is no variation or shadow of turning.*

JAMES 1:17

Perfect Father, Your Word tells me that You hate human pride—that You actively oppose those with arrogant hearts and minds. Lord, remind me often that every good thing I have and accomplish results from Your generosity toward me. The enemy of my soul wants me to believe that I should feel pride over my accomplishments. He wants me to boast about my actions, earnings, and possessions. But all those things are gifts from You, generous Father in heaven. I cannot thank You enough.

NOT TO CONDEMN

"God did not send His Son into the world to condemn the world but that the world might be saved through Him."
JOHN 3:17

So often, Lord, people see the church as judgmental. Many have chosen to evangelize in ways that seem rather harsh. Most don't try to hurt others, but there have been a few casualties along the way. That's why I'm asking You to show me how to speak the truth in love. When I meet people who are living contrary to the way of the gospel, I want to reach out with Your love and grace. But I also need to be true to Your Word. No compromises. Somewhere in the middle of the confusion, there's a way to reach them. I don't know how. . .but You do, Father. What I can't do in the flesh, You can certainly accomplish in the Spirit.

CONFESSION

Whoever confesses that Jesus is the Son of God, God dwells in him, and he in God.
1 John 4:15

Father, I confess that my life is not all that it should be. Even by my own standards, I fall far below what I want to accomplish. I can never be a perfect Christian, and my distress becomes even greater when I compare myself to Jesus.

But Lord, I know my life becomes acceptable to You when I put on the cloak of Jesus. He brings me to righteousness! So I will confess my sins, renew myself in You, and set out refreshed once more, determined to do better.

And a leper came to Him, beseeching Him and kneeling down to Him and saying to Him, "If You are willing, You can make me clean." And moved with compassion, Jesus put out His hand and touched him, and said to him, "I am willing. Be cleansed."
MARK 1:40–41

Dear Father, Jesus had compassion on this man. He cared about the man's problems, and He healed him. I know You care about my problems as well. So teach me to come to You as this man did, with full confidence that You care. . .and that You're able to do all things.

Likewise, may I be a man of compassion too. Help me see others' struggles, and show me how to ease their burdens and let them know of Your mighty love.

WHAT I CANNOT SEE

*For we are saved in hope, but hope
that is seen is not hope. For why does
a man still hope for what he sees?
But if we hope for what we do not see,
then we wait for it with patience.*
ROMANS 8:24–25

This world offers far too many visual images, Lord, and it's nigh impossible to filter them all. By turning on the news, I can see tragedies happening all over the world—hurricanes, riots, war, and so on. It's almost too much to take. But instead of fretting over what I *can* see, I want to have a hope that's based on what I *can't*.

You're in charge. Your plans are mighty to save. So today, I choose to hope for what I don't see, and I will wait patiently as Your will is done.

FAITH DEFINED

Now faith is the substance of things hoped for, the evidence of things not seen. For by it the elders obtained a good report.
HEBREWS 11:1–2

Lord, I know I can't please You without faith. I know I must believe that You are and that You will reward me when I seek after You with everything I have. But sometimes, I still have doubts. Sometimes, I don't feel fully assured that You keep Your promises. Sometimes, I feel like I need to see results before I fully believe. Father, prevent me from becoming discouraged today. I want to continue trusting You and following You with everything I have, knowing that You're working all things out for my good. Thank You for the gift of faith.

EXALTED AMONG THE NATIONS!

"Be still and know that I am God.
I will be exalted among the nations;
I will be exalted in the earth."
Psalm 46:10

This is my prayer, Lord—to see Your name exalted among the nations! Every person in every country is precious to You. And one day, every knee will bow and every tongue will confess that You are Lord. What a day that will be! I can only imagine what it'll be like to see people from every language and tribe lifting Your name together in praise. Until then, show me how I can play a role in exalting You among the nations. I won't cease praying until everyone comes to know You, Lord.

THE MASTER'S VOICE

But you be doers of the word and not hearers only, deceiving your own selves.
JAMES 1:22

Lord, thank You for being kind enough to provide Your Word. Even though the orderliness of nature tells me of Your existence, I would be miserable knowing You had created me and then simply left. I sense Your presence when I read the Bible. Through Your Word, I hear Your voice and learn of Your unbreakable love for me. Your Word gives me a glimpse of You.

Lord, I pray for the will to read Your Word, a mind to understand its meaning, the ability to apply its principles to my life, and the determination to act upon what I learn.

THE NOBLE MAN

*Also the instruments of the scoundrel
are evil. He devises wicked plans to
destroy the poor with lying words, even
when the needy speaks what is right. But
the noble person devises noble plans,
and by noble plans he shall stand.*
ISAIAH 32:7–8

Dear Father, how many scoundrels do I know? It's easy to fall into step with people who gossip, slander, and take pleasure in harming those they don't agree with or don't like. As long as they're nice to me, it's hard for me to see them for who they are. Open my eyes to those whose words and actions are ungodly, and please don't let me become that kind of man. I want to be noble and godly. Make me like You and let all my words and actions be born of love.

MY FUTURE IS SECURE

For by grace you are saved
through faith, and that is not of
yourselves; it is the gift of God.
EPHESIANS 2:8

Heavenly Father, fastening a seat belt pro-vides a sense of safety and security. The same is true with my future, when I believe in Your Son to save me for all eternity. My spiritual seat belt is fastened tight, but I take absolutely no credit for this. You're holding everything in place. When I come to grips with this truth, I don't have to be scared of tomorrow. I can take bold steps into the unknown. I can embrace the adventure. As long as You hold the steering wheel, Father, there's no danger of me veering off course.

VICTORY OVER TEMPTATION

*How shall a young man cleanse his way?
By paying attention to it according to
Your word. With my whole heart I have
sought You. O let me not wander from Your
commandments. Your word have I hidden in
my heart, that I might not sin against You.*

PSALM 119:9–11

Lord Jesus, I want to be able to say no to sin and yes to You. But the enemy of my soul throws so many temptations my way. I know I can have victory by storing up the truth of Your Word in my heart. You showed me how that works when You answered the devil's temptation with scripture. I know that Your Word is a powerful weapon in my war against sin. Remind me to wield it confidently when the enemy tempts me.

ALWAYS JOYFUL

Rejoice always. Pray without ceasing.
1 Thessalonians 5:16–17

If I want to impact my world and make a genuine difference in the lives of those around me, Lord, here's a good place to start! What if, from now on, I responded to every person, situation, and hardship with joy? What if I never stopped praying? What if I made thankfulness a knee-jerk reaction, exuding gratitude for every act of service someone performed on my behalf? Wouldn't this be the best testimony, Father? People would pass by me and say, "I'll have what you're having!" Joy is contagious, after all. Thanks for the reminder, Lord.

VOTING WITH MY WALLET

For we are His workmanship, created in Christ Jesus for good works, which God has before ordained that we should walk in them.
EPHESIANS 2:10

Lord, thank You for the freedom I have to vote both on the local and national level. I pray for Your guidance in carrying out this responsibility.

Similarly, Lord, I will express my convictions about spiritual issues by the choices I make. Help me be responsible in the causes that I choose to support. Guide me in the purchases I make, the businesses I patronize, and the entertainment venues I attend. Heavenly Father, let every vote I cast—either at the polls or with my wallet—make this country a more righteous nation.

FULL ATTENTION

And this is the confidence that we have in Him, that if we ask anything according to His will, He hears us.
1 John 5:14

Dear Father, it's pretty incredible to have an audience with a King, anytime I want it. You've promised that because I'm Your child, I have full access to You. I can talk to You about anything—from minor concerns to life-changing decisions—and You'll listen. As I'm talking, You don't check Your cell phone, scroll through social media, and nod occasionally to make me think You're paying attention. No—when I talk to You, You hang on every word. Thank You for loving me, seeing me as important, and giving full attention to my prayers.

THERE WILL BE A FUTURE

Why are you cast down, O my soul?
And why are you restless in me?
Hope in God, for I shall yet praise
Him for the help of His presence.
Psalm 42:5

Sometimes, I'm struck by a sense of foreboding, Father. My hopes feel dashed. My future seems ruined. And, I confess, I sometimes feel like You've overlooked me in favor of others.

But I know by reading Your Word that there *is* a future for me. This future isn't always easy to see: it takes spiritual wisdom that only You can give. So today, give me the courage to take my best shot and trust You with the rest.

AN ETERNAL HOME

*"In my Father's house are many mansions;
if it were not so, I would have told you. I
go to prepare a place for you. And if I go
and prepare a place for you, I will come
again and receive you to Myself, that
where I am, there you may be also."*
JOHN 14:2–3

Lord Jesus, as You hung dying on a cross of
wood, You took the time to offer an amazing
promise to a penitent criminal: "Today you
shall be with Me in paradise." When I consider
the fact that those words came from the
Creator of the universe, my mind spins. What
will my eternal home look like? Thank You for
preparing a place especially for me—a place
that will be an eternal paradise.

ALL JOY AND PEACE

To be spiritually minded is life and peace.
ROMANS 8:6

I find it interesting, Lord, that joy and peace work hand in hand. When I'm fretting, I have neither. But when I put my trust in You—when I count on You to handle the things I can't— then I'm at peace. This brings an indescribable level of joy. . .which is just what You want for me. According to Your Word, You want me to overflow by the power of Your Spirit as I trust in You. This is an intentional move on Your part—and I know You do it because my joy has the power to change others. So fill me up, Lord!

SUPPLICATION

Be anxious for nothing, but in everything, by prayer and supplication with thanksgiving, let your requests be made known to God.
PHILIPPIANS 4:6

Father, I'm aware of many people who are suffering and who are in difficult situations. I pray that they and their families will be able to work out the difficulty. Help me find a way to ease their burden.

I pray also for those who live lives of quiet desperation—those who never reveal their distress but suffer in silent hopelessness. I pray that I will be sensitive to these individuals, recognize their concerns, and take action to relieve them of the suffering they are trying to bear alone.

PREACHING TO THE WORLD

*It pleased God, who separated me from
my mother's womb and called me by
His grace, to reveal His Son in me, that I
might preach Him among the nations.*
GALATIANS 1:15–16

I'm not the apostle Paul, Lord Jesus—not even close. But I do know that, in a sense, this verse applies to me too. The moment I accepted You, I committed myself to a life of service. Everywhere I go, I'm called to tell others how amazing You are. Whether this means explicitly sharing the gospel or showing Your love to strangers at the supermarket, I want to follow this command. Give me opportunities today to preach You to the world.

NEW COMPASSIONS EVERY DAY

It is because of the LORD's mercies that we are not consumed, because His compassions do not fail. They are new every morning. Your faithfulness is great.
LAMENTATIONS 3:22–23

Lord, I understand why You don't want me to go to bed angry. You don't want the woes of one day to spill over into the next. When I fall asleep calm, I can awake to new beginnings. In the same way, I'm grateful that You don't go to bed angry with me when I've had a less than stellar day. You love me, forgive me, and promise that Your compassions will be new tomorrow morning. What a faithful God You are. Left to my own devices, I'd be stuck in the angst of today. But with You, my future is secure because Your compassions never fail. Thank You, Lord.

ASKING FOR A MIRACLE

*Jesus said to him, "If you can believe,
all things are possible to him who
believes." And immediately the father of
the child cried out and said with tears,
"Lord, I believe; help my unbelief."*
MARK 9:23–24

Lord Jesus, I've read of the amazing miracles You performed during Your earthly ministry, and I've heard modern-day stories that can only be explained as being Your work. I know You have the power to perform miracles on behalf of anyone who cries out to You—but it's sometimes hard to believe that this applies to me too. Thank You for loving me and making me one of Your own. Jesus, please help my unbelief.

AFFECTING ETERNITY

"God so loved the world that He gave His only begotten Son, that whoever believes in Him should not perish but have everlasting life."
JOHN 3:16

It's sobering to think that my actions could affect eternity, but I know it's true. My attitude today could sway someone—either to a lifetime with You or to a decision to avoid Christianity altogether. This is one reason I pursue a holy, godly life—because I know You long for me to be a good representation of You while I have the chance. So don't let me waste a moment, Lord! Shift my focus from myself to others—from a life of self-gain to a life of giving. Here's to spending a lifetime in heaven with the people I impact today.

EXHILARATING FREEDOM

Jesus answered them, "Truly, truly, I say to you, whoever commits sin is the servant of sin. And the servant does not abide in the house forever, but the Son abides forever. Therefore if the Son shall make you free, you shall be free indeed."
JOHN 8:34–36

Lord Jesus, life without You would be pointless, frustrating, and ultimately hopeless. I'd be trapped by my own sinful nature, forever trying to improve but never able to make any progress. But because of Your Spirit that dwells in me, I'm moving forward each day in my walk with You. And as sin's slavery shrinks into a distant memory, my view of my eternal home in heaven with You grows larger and larger each day. Thank You for giving me such exhilarating freedom!

THE FIRST ONE TO CALL

It is better to trust in the LORD than to put
confidence in man. It is better to trust in
the LORD than to put confidence in princes.
PSALM 118:8–9

All-powerful Father, I have a list of family members, friends, and acquaintances which I consult whenever I need help with a problem. While this isn't necessarily a bad thing, other people should never be my first source of comfort or relief. When I need a refuge, You are the only place to turn. People are flawed. They get busy, and they might forget me. You, on the other hand, are strong and mighty, eternal in Your love. Next time I need help, before I pick up my phone to call a friend, remind me to run to You.

WIDE VISION

It's such a relief to know that Your vision is wide, Father. You can see from one end of the universe to the other—from every star to every planet to the next breath I'm going to take. You see it all and orchestrate it with Your majestic hand. And because I know Your vision is complete, I can count on You to lead and guide. If You can see what's hiding beyond the farthest star, surely You can see what the future holds for me. Thank You, Lord!

THE PERIL OF LOVING MONEY

But those who will be rich fall into temptation and a snare, and into many foolish and hurtful lusts, which drown men in destruction and perdition. For the love of money is the root of all evil, which while some coveted after, they have gone astray from the faith and pierced themselves through with many sorrows.

1 Timothy 6:9–10

Father in heaven, I've seen so many people destroy their lives—and the lives of others—by their love of money. Lord, You never condemned money itself as evil, and You actually encourage men to work hard to earn a living. But too many of us focus more on loving money than on using it as a tool to care for others and fund Your work. Empower me to work hard to earn, but keep my heart from the love of money.

THIS IS ETERNAL LIFE

"And this is life eternal, that they might know You, the only true God, and Jesus Christ whom You have sent."

JOHN 17:3

There is no eternal life without You, God. No one enters heaven's gates without coming to a saving relationship with Your Son. That's why it's so important that I let people know. It's not enough to just assume people are ready for heaven—I have to know for sure. Show me how to go about this, I pray. I don't want to put up any walls or cause division. Make my words grace-filled so that I may be most effective. At every opportunity, I will proclaim Your goodness, Lord. . .and then I'll watch You move.

SPIRITUAL SIBLINGS

Do we not all have one Father? Has not one God created us? Why do we act treacherously, every man against his brother, by profaning the covenant of our fathers?
MALACHI 2:10

Good Father, one of the worst forms of betrayal is the kind that occurs between siblings. Jealousy arises where love should flourish. Hatred usurps the place of compassion. Trust turns instantly to bitterness and regret. How much more terrible is such a betrayal when it occurs among the children of God. Lord, help me to get along with my brothers and sisters in Christ, giving and receiving strength as we walk with You. I want to show my spiritual siblings the love You've shown toward me.

CHILDLIKE

*"Whoever humbles himself like this
little child, the same is greatest
in the kingdom of heaven."*
MATTHEW 18:4

Perfect God, humility can be hard for a man. We're taught to be strong and self-confident. Those are biblical qualities, but they can easily get mixed with pride. Jesus was strong and self-confident, but He was also humble, placing Himself completely under Your authority and obedient even to death. He put others' needs before His own. Teach me to be humble like that. Give me the confidence to love with abandon, like a child. Teach me to trust You completely and to place myself under Your authority. And teach me to put others' needs before my own. May there be less of me and more of You.

BROKEN CHAINS

Then they cried to the LORD in their trouble, and He saved them out of their distresses. He brought them out of darkness and the shadow of death, and broke their chains in pieces. Oh that men would praise the LORD. . . ! For He has broken the gates of bronze and cut the bars of iron in pieces.
PSALM 107:13–16

What a picture of Your power, Lord! You've broken through gates of bronze and bars of iron to get to me. Even when I was in my deepest, darkest place, You came barreling through, ready to release my chains and give me a future. That's the kind of unfailing love You have for me. You've always wanted to lift me to higher places. I praise You for the great, inspiring passion You have for Your children.

KNOWING THE ENEMY

Be sober and vigilant, because your adversary the devil walks about like a roaring lion, seeking whom he may devour. Resist him, steadfast in the faith, knowing that the same afflictions are experienced by your brothers who are in the world.

1 PETER 5:8-9

Father in heaven, thank You for the heads-up about the enemy of my soul, the devil. He loves to use lies and temptations to derail my walk with You. He knows that I am Yours forever, so now he works overtime to keep me from the work You've given me to do. Lord, give me the insight and wisdom to know when the devil is lying in wait so that I may avoid him and remain on track for You.

MORE LIKE YOU

*That they all may be one, as You, Father,
are in Me, and I in You, that they also
may be one in Us, that the world may
believe that You have sent Me."*
JOHN 17:21

Father, it's remarkable how long-time married couples anticipate one another's needs and communicate with merely a nod or a gesture. In some cases, they even start to look alike.

I pray that such closeness will define my relationship with You. I want to absorb Your Word so thoroughly that Your will becomes a part of me. I want prayer to become second-nature. And most of all, I pray that I'll have the same spiritual characteristics as You.

REMIND ME

For we are His workmanship, created in Christ Jesus for good works, which God has before ordained that we should walk in them.
EPHESIANS 2:10

Father, it's sometimes easy to forget that You created me with a purpose—that I'm not just a random combination of cells and DNA. You planned my life with specific goals in mind. Those tasks involve good works designed to help others and point them to You. You placed me in just the right place so that I can live out my part of Your plan. As I go about my day, remind me to do good works. Remind me to be patient, kind, generous, and cheerful. Remind me to show grace where it's not deserved. Remind me to love.

TO THE END

*"And behold, I am with you always,
even to the end of the world."*
MATTHEW 28:20

It's probably a good thing that I don't know how long I'll live, Lord. Instead of spending my time counting down the minutes, I'm free to live each day with purpose, ready to see Your plans fulfilled in my life. Best of all, I can enjoy this path toward spiritual maturity. No matter how many years I have left, I'll spend each one following You. How remarkable to know that the Creator of the universe cares enough about me to walk with me every day of my life.

TEMPTED TO COMPROMISE

"If it be so, our God whom we serve is able to deliver us from the burning fiery furnace. . . . But if not, let it be known to you, O king, that we will not serve your gods, nor worship the golden statue that you have set up."

DANIEL 3:17–18

Righteous Father, thank You for this example of men who refused to compromise on what they knew was right. I need their encouragement in a world that continually pressures me to violate my conscience. When I'm faced with a choice between honoring You or compromising my faith, give me the courage to stand for You. Lord, I will serve and obey You and You alone, even when it means facing all sorts of difficulties.

MONEY MATTERS

For the love of money is the root of all evil, which while some coveted after, they have gone astray from the faith and pierced themselves through with many sorrows.

1 TIMOTHY 6:10

Lord, deliver me from desiring the riches of this world. Protect me from the evils that stem from chasing inordinate wealth. May I never compromise my service to You by trusting my bank account to protect my future. Father, I do desire health and prosperity, but You are the only good Shepherd who can lead me to eternal blessings. May my faith stay grounded in You so that my mind and heart will not be overtaken with greed. May I remain aware of Satan's tactics to turn blessings into reproach. Give me wisdom to be a trusting steward.

INCLUSIVE

And He came and preached peace to you who were afar off and to those who were near. For through Him we both have access by one Spirit to the Father. Now therefore you are no longer strangers and foreigners but fellow citizens with the saints and of the household of God.

EPHESIANS 2:17–19

Father, people are infatuated with the word *inclusion*. But You were inclusive long before I was born. Even though You called Your people—Israel—to be Your own, You also called the Gentiles to partake of Your love. Teach me Your kind of inclusiveness, Father. Help me see all people as objects of Your love. Help me show them Your kindness and grace. Make my life a magnet of Your presence, drawing all people to You.

VICTORY!

But thanks be to God, who gives us the victory through our Lord Jesus Christ. Therefore, my beloved brothers, be steadfast, immovable, always abounding in the work of the Lord, since you know that your labor is not in vain in the Lord.
1 CORINTHIANS 15:57–58

I love a good victory, Jesus, whether it's in sports, at election time, or a game with a friend. But there's an even greater victory than these: Your death on the cross. Because You won the ultimate victory over sin and death, all who call on Your name can obtain eternal life. How can I ever thank You enough for winning that battle on my behalf, Lord? I commit myself to enthusiastically sharing the good news of what You've done so that others can share in this victory too.

THE PRIVILEGE OF PRAYER

"Moreover, as for me, God forbid that I should sin against the LORD in ceasing to pray for you. But I will teach you the good and right way."
1 SAMUEL 12:23

Faithful God, thank You for the gift of prayer. Prayer is an awesome privilege for the man who loves You, but it's also my responsibility. You've called me to pray about *everything*—myself, my family, my Christian brothers and sisters, those who need Jesus, my nation and its leaders, and anything else You lay on my heart. When I pray, You start changing hearts and situations. May I never neglect my daily talks with You—or fail to hear what You say in return.

"Give, and it shall be given to you. . . .
For with the same measure that you use,
it shall be measured back to you."
LUKE 6:38

Lord Jesus, You set the standard for generosity by giving up Your life for a sinful world. May I always be reminded of Your sacrifice when I see a need that I can fill. Just as a farmer plants seeds and profits from the harvest, You also bless those who share their assets with pure motives, not out of a selfish expectation of reward. I want to be Your hand extended toward those who have physical, spiritual, and financial needs.

WORTHY

I, therefore, the prisoner of the Lord, beseech you to walk worthy of the vocation to which you are called, with all lowliness and meekness, with long-suffering, forbearing one another in love, endeavoring to keep the unity of the Spirit in the bond of peace.
EPHESIANS 4:1–3

Dear Father, as I read these words, I can't help but think of times I don't walk worthy of the vocation to which I am called. But You didn't just call me—You equipped me. You've given me everything I need to act with humility, gentleness, patience, and love. Through Your Holy Spirit, I have what is necessary to live in unity and peace with those around me. Though others may or may not live according to Your will, I want to do my part. Help me live in a way that's worthy of a man who is called Your son.

A STRONG SUPPORT

"For the eyes of the LORD run to and fro throughout the whole earth, to show Himself strong on behalf of those whose heart is committed to Him."

2 CHRONICLES 16:9

It's fascinating, Lord, to think that You can see the whole universe—every planet, continent, country, city, neighborhood, and home—all at once. I marvel at the very idea. It encourages me to know that You're watching Your children so that You can bring strength. Please keep watching me today, Father. Give me the strength I need to travel down this road You've placed me on. Thanks for keeping such a good eye on me, Lord.

PLANTING THE RIGHT SEEDS

Do not be deceived; God is not mocked,
for whatever a man sows, that he shall also
reap. For he who sows to his flesh shall of the
flesh reap corruption, but he who sows to the
Spirit shall of the Spirit reap life everlasting.
GALATIANS 6:7–8

Righteous God, You've arranged life on this earth so that a man's thoughts and actions have consequences. I know that if I live and think according to Your will, I'll see good results. . .and if I don't, I won't. Lord, I want to reap the harvest of eternal life—not just for myself but for those You've placed in my life. Keep me mindful of the importance of living the way You've called me to live, and not in a way that satisfies my own desires.

TIME MANAGEMENT

See then that you walk carefully, not as fools, but as wise, redeeming the time because the days are evil. Therefore do not be unwise, but understand what the will of the Lord is.
EPHESIANS 5:15–17

Dear Father, "the days are evil." That's a great way to describe what's happening in the world right now. Everywhere I look, there is anger. There's social and political unrest. There's much division and little unity. Now more than ever, I need Your wisdom. I need to make every minute count for Your kingdom because I feel our time is growing short. I don't want to waste a single day. Make Your will clear for my life, Father, and help me walk in wisdom, godliness, and love. As long as I have breath in this world, let me honor You.

YOU STRETCHED OUT THE HEAVENS

He has made the earth by His power;
He has established the world by His
wisdom and has stretched out the
heavens by His understanding.
JEREMIAH 51:15

Lord, I can almost picture Your mighty hand grabbing the corners of heaven and tugging them into place. You stretched, and all things were established. The same has been true in my life, Lord. Your plans are stretching me beyond my initial capabilities. Your wisdom is growing me into a man who trusts You more and looks hopefully toward the future. How can I ever thank You enough for growing me into a stronger man of God?

A PROPER SELF-IMAGE

For through the grace given to me I say to every man who is among you not to think of himself more highly than he ought to think, but to think soberly, according to the measure of faith God has dealt to every man.

ROMANS 12:3

Heavenly Father, it's tempting to think more highly of myself than You would have me think. You don't call me to think self-abasing thoughts but to consider myself as a sinner saved through Your Son's work on the cross. In light of that, help me to remember that any good in me flows from You and You alone. Thank You for loving me and bringing me into Your eternal kingdom. May I always remember that none of the glory belongs to me.

PRESS ON

*Not as though I had already attained,
or were already perfect, but I follow after,
if that I may apprehend that for which
also I am apprehended of Christ Jesus.*
PHILIPPIANS 3:12

Almighty Father, it's sometimes hard to keep going. Some days, it feels like life itself is against me, and I don't know how I'll move forward. Thank You for this reminder that You're not finished with me. This race of life is worth the struggle because I know You'll be waiting at the end. You are my prize, Lord—not only in the life to come but in life of blessings I live today. I know I have a long way to go, but I will press on. Thank You for making each day worth living.

*"And when you stand praying, forgive,
if you have anything against anyone,
that your Father who is in heaven may
also forgive you for your trespasses."*
MARK 11:25

Faithful, forgiving God, I never want anything to come between us. I never want to feel as if my line of communication with You is broken or damaged in any way. I know You want me to forgive those who have hurt or offended me—even if they don't confess their wrongdoing—and I know that my lack of forgiveness can keep You from hearing me. Help me to freely forgive so that You can forgive me and respond to my prayers. If I'm harboring bitterness against anyone, bring it to my mind so that I can forgive that person today.

ADJUSTING THE SCHEDULE

For we hear that there are some who walk among you disorderly, not working at all, but are busybodies. Now those who are such we command and exhort by our Lord Jesus Christ that with quietness they work and eat their own bread.

2 Thessalonians 3:11–12

Father, I don't want to be a busybody. Yet it's easy to get caught up in idle talk that doesn't do anything to build others up. It's easy to waste hours on social media each day while spending mere minutes with You. Forgive me for spending time in such fruitless activities. Life is too short to waste on trivial things. Help me focus on the work You've set before me—loving others and shining Your light in this dark world.

HEARING AND DOING

But you be doers of the word and not hearers only, deceiving your own selves.
JAMES 1:22

Lord God, I confess that I don't always act on what I read in Your Word. Sometimes, I see some great truth. . .but then go about my day as if I've forgotten what I've read. Please forgive me. I know You want me to read the Bible every day, but I also know reading means little if it doesn't change my actions. Through Your Spirit, bring the Word to life in my soul so that I can do what it says.

BEYOND COMPREHENSION

"What is man, that You are mindful of him, or the son of man, that You care for him? You made him a little lower than the angels. You crowned him with glory and honor and set him over the works of Your hands. You have put all things in subjection under his feet."

HEBREWS 2:6–8

Good Father, when I compare Your glory to my smallness, I feel overwhelmed. I can't understand why You think of me at all. Yet because You are love personified, You've chosen me as the object of Your affection. You made me in Your image and called me Your son. You reside in my heart and grant me full access to Your power, wisdom, mercy, and grace. Though I don't understand it, I accept it. I want my life to honor You and point others to Your love.

PERFECT TIMING

*The Lord is not slow concerning His
promise, as some men count slowness,
but is long-suffering toward us, not
willing that any should perish but that
all should come to repentance.*
2 PETER 3:9

Sovereign God, Your timing isn't like my
timing. You exist outside of any human time
constraints, and You alone control the timing
of all the events leading to Christ's return. I
want Him to come back soon to set all things
right and establish His eternal kingdom. But
You, being the perfect example of love, want
to first give everyone a chance to turn to
You. Help me to plan ahead as if I know Jesus
won't return soon. . .but to work and live as
if He's coming back today. Either way, You
win—and so do I.

EARTHLY AUTHORITY

Let every soul be subject to the governing authorities. For there is no authority but by God, and the authorities that exist are ordained by God. Therefore whoever resists authority resists the ordinance of God, and those who resist shall receive condemnation for themselves.

ROMANS 13:1–2

Lord of lords, thank You for placing people in positions of authority so that they can keep order in the world. I know You've appointed those rulers, even those with whom I disagree. I also know You want me to live in obedience to earthly laws as long as doing so doesn't cause me to disobey You. Help me know the difference between laws that are compatible with Your commands and those that are not.

ALWAYS PRESENT

Where shall I go from Your Spirit? Or where shall I flee from Your presence? If I ascend up into heaven, You are there. If I make my bed in hell, behold, You are there.

PSALM 139:7–8

Lord, I'm grateful that it's impossible to escape Your presence—that because of Your deep, personal love, You'll never leave me on my own. Even when I attempt to go it alone, You are there. Even when I don't feel Your presence, You are there. Even when I wonder if You've abandoned me, You are there. Even when I'm tempted to sin—and even when I give in to that temptation—You are there, drawing me back to You.

TOPICAL INDEX

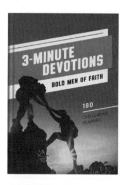